# MICROWAVE

# *Mug Cakes!*

# MICROWAVE

# Mug Cakes!

## 40 home-made treats in an instant

### HANNAH MILES

photography by Clare Winfield

LORENZ BOOKS

# CONTENTS

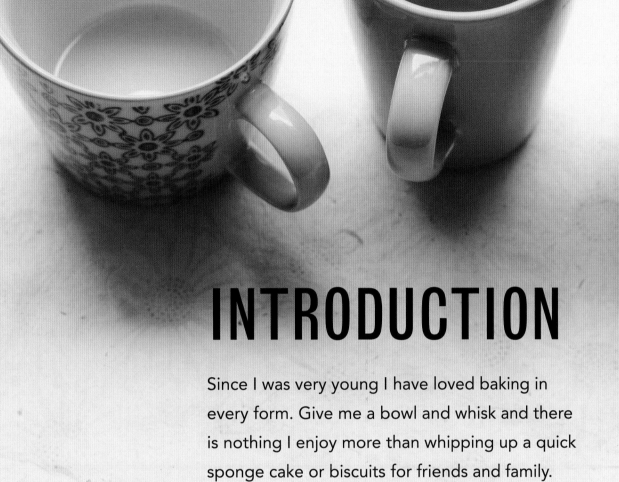

# INTRODUCTION

Since I was very young I have loved baking in every form. Give me a bowl and whisk and there is nothing I enjoy more than whipping up a quick sponge cake or biscuits for friends and family. I recognize though that traditional baking takes time and sometimes all you need is a quick fix of cake. This is where microwave mug cakes come into their own. They are remarkably moist and delicious and can be prepared in less than 5 minutes. The cakes in this book are perfect for those evenings when you get in from work and need something sweet to unwind with in front of the TV or for hungry children after a long day at school.

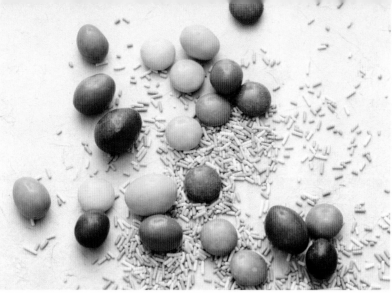

# TREATS IN AN INSTANT!

This book contains a multitude of treats you can prepare in an instant. Favourite cakes, such as carrot cake with cream cheese frosting, Victoria sponge cake and delicious chocolate cakes are all included, but also new twists such as gin and lemon drizzle cake, salted caramel pudding and pistachio and white chocolate cake. For those want an American classic, there are recipes for the red velvet and the ever-popular spiced pumpkin cake or rocky road mug cake, bursting with cherries, marshmallow and chocolate.

The microwave also makes perfect sponge puddings which taste exactly like steamed puddings, but that can be prepared in a fraction of the time. Pineapple upside down sponge is one of my favourites, or why not try a syrup sponge or one rich with lemon curd, all mouthwatering served with lashings of custard or cream.

If you love fruit then the Fruity Cups chapter in this book contains juicy cranberry and clementine cake, banana walnut and pretzel cake and even a succulent pear and chocolate cake containing a whole pear filled with a chocolate centre.

As microwave cakes are very easy to prepare with no hot ovens, they are great for children to make themselves, with very little adult supervision required. The only time to take care is when removing the cooked cake from the microwave as sometimes the mugs can be hot. Although most of the recipes in this book are suitable for children, there are some fun cakes for them to make in the Just for Kids chapter, including a sweet cola bottle cake and a pink marshmallow cake.

For last-minute celebrations, the final chapter of this book contains quick and easy cakes for every festivity – from cute pumpkins for Thanksgiving and colourful cakes for Halloween to a miniature chocolate log for Christmas with a dusting of icing sugar snow, and a mini birthday cake.

The method for making a mug cake is very quick and simple – just whisk everything together in one bowl and then bake in the microwave – no creaming of butter and sugar together or folding in of flour. The recipe below is for a classic vanilla cake batter – which you can then easily transform with flavours of your choosing. It is the base batter for all the cakes in this book, so once you have mastered it you can bake to your heart's delight.

# BASIC PLAIN MUG CAKE

Place the butter in a microwaveproof bowl in the microwave and heat on full power for about 40 seconds until it has melted then leave it to cool.

Place the flour, sugar, milk, egg, vanilla and melted butter in a mixing bowl and whisk together until everything is incorporated. Make sure that there are no lumps of flour. The batter should be thick and runny.

Pour the batter into the mug until it is no more than two-thirds full. Do not overfill the mug otherwise it may overflow when cooking.

Cook on full power in a microwave (850W) for 3 minutes until the cake springs back to your touch. Leave to cool for a few minutes, then tuck into your delicious cake. This cake must be eaten on the day it is made.

SERVES: 1
PREPARATION TIME: 5 minutes
COOKING TIME: 3 minutes
    (850W microwave)
EQUIPMENT: 1 microwave-
    proof mug (400ml/
    15fl oz/1½ cups), whisk

45g/1½oz/2 tbsp butter
60g/2oz/3 tbsp self-raising/
    self-rising flour, sifted
60g/2oz/2 tbsp caster/
    superfine sugar
30ml/1fl oz/2 tbsp milk
20g/¾oz/1 tbsp beaten egg
5ml/1tsp vanilla extract

## BASIC INGREDIENTS

Only a few ingredients are required for making mug cakes – just self-raising/self-rising flour, sugar, butter, egg and milk and then flavourings of your choosing. If you do not have self-raising flour you can make your own using 5ml/1 tsp of baking powder to every 100g/3½oz of plain/all-purpose flour and sift together.

It is best to use good quality ingredients, as this will result in a better flavour. For example, the golden yolks of organic free-range eggs will give a wonderful golden sponge. The recipes use 20g/¾oz/1 tbsp beaten egg, which is about half an egg, so keep the remainder for something else (or another mug cake!).

Vanilla extract is another ingredient that it is worth splashing out on as pure extract gives a much stronger flavour. Indulgent vanilla bean powder can also be used and gives an intense vanilla perfume to your cakes.

For those who are allergic to gluten, making quick cakes can be problematic and this is where the microwave comes into its own. This basic gluten-free cake is delicious and is ready in just 2½ minutes, meaning that those with wheat allergies don't have to miss out. You can substitute this recipe for most of the recipes in this book. It is really important to check that the other ingredients in the recipe are also gluten-free though. Chocolate and cocoa powders can contain wheat and some dried fruits and icing/confectioners' sugars contain anti-caking agents which can be wheat-based. Always check the ingredients carefully. When substituting this recipe note the reduced cooking time.

# BASIC GLUTEN-FREE MUG CAKE

**SERVES: 1**
**PREPARATION TIME: 5 minutes**
**COOKING TIME: 2½ minutes**
(850W microwave)
**EQUIPMENT: 1 microwave-**
proof mug (400ml/
15fl oz/1½ cups), whisk

45g/1½oz/2 tbsp butter
60g/2oz/3 tbsp gluten-free
self-raising/self-rising flour,
sifted
60g/2oz/2 tbsp caster/
superfine sugar
30ml/1fl oz/2 tbsp milk
20g/¾oz/1 tbsp beaten egg
5ml/1 tsp vanilla extract

Place the butter in a microwaveproof bowl in the microwave and heat on full power for about 40 seconds until it has melted then leave it to cool.

Place the gluten-free flour, sugar, milk, egg, vanilla and melted butter in a mixing bowl and whisk together until everything is incorporated. Make sure that there are no lumps of flour. The batter should be thick and runny.

Pour the batter into the mug until it is no more than two-thirds full. Do not overfill the mug otherwise it may overflow when cooking.

Cook on full power in a microwave (850W) for about 2½ minutes until the cake springs back to your touch. The gluten-free sponge takes less time to cook than the basic sponge recipe. Leave to cool for a few minutes before eating. This cake must be eaten on the day it is made.

## VARIATION FOR MUG PUDDING SPONGE
For a gluten-free pudding sponge, in recipes such as the pineapple upside down pudding or sponge pudding with jam, syrup or lemon curd, replace the flour with gluten-free flour or ground almonds and baking powder.

Lactose- and dairy-free allergy intolerance can mean that people have to avoid cake, given the butter content. These quick and easy sponges are made with oil or lactose-free spread and dairy-free milk such as soya or almond milk. Other dairy-free milks work well. This recipe can be substituted for the basic cake batters throughout this book, provided that the recipe does not call for cream or other dairy products. This is a great recipe for whipping up a dairy-free sponge in no time at all.

# BASIC LACTOSE-/DAIRY-FREE MUG CAKE

SERVES: 1
PREPARATION TIME: 5 minutes
COOKING TIME: 3 minutes
   (850W microwave)
EQUIPMENT: 1 microwave-
   proof mug (400ml/
   15fl oz/1½ cups), whisk

60g/2oz/3 tbsp self-raising/
   self-rising flour, sifted
60g/2oz/2 tbsp caster/
   superfine sugar

20g/¾oz/1 tbsp beaten egg
30ml/1fl oz/2 tbsp almond milk
   or rice milk
5ml/1tsp vanilla extract
45g/1½oz/2 tbsp lactose-free
   spread (for the lactose-free
   cake) or 30ml/2 tbsp
   vegetable oil (for the dairy-
   free cake)
5ml/1 tsp vanilla extract

If you are making a lactose-free version of this cake, place the lactose-free spread in a microwaveproof bowl in the microwave and heat on full power for about 40 seconds until it has melted then leave it to cool.

Place the flour, sugar, egg, almond or rice milk, vanilla and melted lactose-free spread or the oil (depending on whether you are making a lactose-free or dairy-free version of this cake) in a mixing bowl and whisk together until everything is incorporated. Make sure that there are no lumps of flour. The batter should be thick and runny.

Pour the batter into the mug until it is no more than two-thirds full. Do not overfill the mug otherwise it may overflow when cooking.

Cook on full power in a microwave (850W) for 3 minutes until the cake springs back to your touch. Leave to cool for a few minutes, then tuck into your delicious cake. This cake must be eaten on the day it is made.

## BASIC MICROWAVE KNOW-HOW

Every microwave is different and it is important to get to know your own microwave. All the recipes in this book are for a standard 850W microwave and generally take 3 minutes to cook on full power. If you have a differently powered microwave you will need to adjust the cooking times up for a lower powered microwave or down for a higher powered. It is best to ascertain the cooking time for your microwave by making a test cake and checking the cake after 2 minutes, then cooking for a further 30 seconds and checking again, repeating as necessary until the cake is cooked. This is when the sponge springs bake to your touch and the cake batter is no longer sticky. The cake will continue to cook in the hot mug once removed from the microwave so be careful not to overcook.

## ADAPTING FOR LARGER QUANTITIES

Microwave cakes can easily be scaled up by doubling or tripling the recipe quantities and then baking in the number of mugs that you have increased the size of the recipe by – i.e. if you triple the recipe quantity bake the cake batter in three mugs.

It is best to cook the mugs one at the time. If you cook more than one mug together you will need to increase the cooking time to allow the double quantity of batter to cook.

It is hard to scale down the recipe in terms of making the batter, although of course you could make two smaller mugs from the batter and reduce the cooking time.

## WHAT IS A MUG AND HOW MUCH TO FILL IT?

It is possible to bake a microwave cake in any type of microwave-safe mug or container. The recipe quantities in this book are all designed for a 400ml/15fl oz/1½ cup mug and it is important not to overfill your mug otherwise it will lead to a messy microwave. I know this from experience! As a general rule of thumb, you must fill your chosen container no more than two-thirds full otherwise the cake batter may overflow when baking. If you use a smaller mug then just put less of the cake batter in, or line with baking parchment following the instructions on page 19 to enable the cake to cook above the sides of the mug without overflowing. You can cook the cakes in a microwaveproof bowl or microwaveproof silicon mould if you prefer.

You can bake these cakes in any type of mug that is microwaveproof. Glass mugs can also be used. (Do not use mugs with any metal element or decoration.) Take care when removing the mug from the microwave as it may be hot. The mug you use may also have an impact on cooking time. For example a thicker mug may mean a longer cooking time is needed.

Although the recipes suggest making the batter in a separate bowl, you can mix the batter in the mug itself. Make sure that you wipe the top of the mug clean with a cloth after mixing, before cooking.

## STORAGE

Microwave cakes unfortunately do not last and need to be eaten soon after being made. This is not really an issue as they are so quick to prepare so it is best to make them just before you want to eat. If you are not going to eat the cake straight away, store it in an airtight container. If you make a sponge pudding and want to reheat it after it has gone cold, you can do this by microwaving it for up to 20 seconds to rewarm it, but this is not really recommended as it can lead to the cake being overcooked.

# LINING AND TURNING OUT CAKES

Although it is not necessary to line the mug when you are making a microwave mug cake, this can prevent the cakes overspilling. Also, if you want to turn the cake out to serve inverted (such as the syrup sponge pudding or the pineapple upside down pudding) or to decorate (such as the chocolate log or Halloween cake) then lining the mug with baking parchment makes it very easy to remove the cake to serve.

To do this, cut a piece of baking parchment into a rectangle about 2.5cm/1in taller than your mug and slightly wider than the circumference of your mug. Grease the mug with a little butter and place the baking parchment inside so that it lies flat around the sides of the mug with a little paper overlapping at the join. Pour the batter into the mug. The batter will push the paper tight against the side of the mug. Bake the cake following the instructions in the recipe and then, once cooked, remove the lining paper. To remove the cake from the mug, slide a knife around the inside of the mug and then invert the mug to turn the cake out.

Sometimes, microwave cakes can overflow over the side of a mug when the batter cooks and using the above lining paper method avoids this happening, as the cake can cook higher than the sides of the mug. Leave the cake to cool for a few minutes before removing the lining paper. If greased it will slide out easily.

If you need to line a round-bottomed tea cup, cut out a 5cm/2in slit into the bottom half of the baking parchment. Grease the cup well and then insert the paper so that the bottom fringes of the paper overlap and fit snugly into the bottom of the cup. Press them down with your fingertips, if you need to.

If you are not lining the mug, you do not need to grease it.

## LINING PAPER

There are various different names for lining paper, such as greaseproof, waxed, baking paper and baking parchment. Greaseproof is ideal for wrapping foods for storage. Baking parchment has a silicone lining that prevents cakes from sticking to it and so it is best for using with the recipes in this book. Do not use silver foil, or any metal object, as it will cause sparks in the microwave.

## ADAPTING FLAVOURS

One of the best things about mug cakes is the simplicity of varying flavours. Once you have mastered the basic cake and pudding batters above you can adapt them in hundreds of ways. A little grated citrus zest is delicious, or a handful or chopped nuts gives great flavour and texture. Chocolate chips are always a winning addition or a little coffee or peppermint extract give instant flavour.

For richer cakes with more caramel flavours, you can use muscovado/molasses or soft dark brown sugars instead of caster/superfine sugar. Spices also add delicate flavours – ground cinnamon, ground ginger, nutmeg or even unusual spices, such as caraway seeds.

Dried fruit such as raisins, sultanas/golden raisins or currants, dried cranberries or apricots will add texture to your cakes. However, if you a making a gluten-free version check the ingredients carefully to ensure they don't contain any wheat-based anti-caking agent.

You can even make savoury cakes by omitting the sugar and adding a little grated cheese and mustard.

## ADDING TOPPINGS AND DECORATIONS

Although these are quick and easy cakes to make, there is no reason not to enjoy decorating the cakes for a special occasion. You can top cakes with glacé icing, tinted with a few drops of food colouring for a pretty effect. Alternatively pipe a large swirl of buttercream or cream cheese frosting on top, to create a great alternative to the popular cupcake. Once iced the cakes can be made to look extra-special with the addition of sugar sprinkles and sugar decorations. If you are making gluten-free or dairy-free cakes, always check the ingredient on any decorations carefully to ensure that they are safe to use.

For a simple decoration, use a swivel peeler and create chocolate curls by pulling the peeler along the edge of the bar of chocolate. You can do this with plain/semisweet, milk or white chocolate. Store-bought sweets and candies also make for yummy decorations that kids will love.

# CLASSIC CAKES

In this chapter you will find recipes for all your favourite classic cakes, such as coffee and walnut, the ever-popular American red velvet with delicious cream cheese frosting, and even a five-minute carrot cake decorated with sugar carrots. For chocolate lovers, there are two special treats: rocky road cake bursting with marshmallows and cherries, and a scrumptious chocolate chip marshmallow cake!

Pearl sugar is the classic sugar crystals that are added to Belgian waffles to give them a sugary crunch. They are perfect on top of cakes – whether baked in the microwave or the oven as they make a crispy sugary top. This is a very plain and simple cake but it tastes delicious and is lovely served with a handful of ripe berries on the side.

# PEARL SUGAR VANILLA CAKE

SERVES: 1
PREPARATION TIME: 5 minutes
COOKING TIME: 3 minutes
    (850W microwave)
EQUIPMENT: 1 microwave-
    proof mug (400ml/
    15fl oz/1½ cups), whisk,
    baking parchment

45g/1½oz/2 tbsp butter, plus
    extra for greasing

60g/2oz/3 tbsp self-raising/
    self-rising flour, sifted
60g/2oz/2 tbsp caster/
    superfine sugar
30ml/1fl oz/2 tbsp milk
20g/¾oz/1 tbsp beaten egg
5ml/1 tsp vanilla bean paste or
    vanilla extract
28g/1oz/1 tbsp pearl sugar
    crystals
Fresh berries to serve

Place the butter in a heatproof bowl in the microwave and heat on full power for about 40 seconds until it has melted then leave it to cool.

Place the flour, sugar, milk, egg and vanilla bean paste into the bowl with the melted butter, and whisk together until everything is incorporated. Make sure that there are no lumps of flour. The batter should be thick and runny.

Cut a piece of baking parchment into a rectangle about 2.5cm/1in taller than your mug and slightly wider than the circumference of your mug. Grease the mug with a little butter and place the baking parchment inside so that it lies flat around the sides of the mug with a little paper overlapping at the join.

Pour the batter into the mug. Cook on full power in a microwave (850W) for 2 minutes 30 seconds until the cake springs back to your touch. Carefully remove the cake from the microwave and sprinkle the top of the cake with the pearl sugar crystals. Return to the microwave and cook on full power for a further 30 seconds. If you have a different power microwave, use the cooking time adjustment instructions on page 16.

Leave the cake to cool slightly before serving or leave to cool completely, serving with fresh berries if you wish. Remove the lining paper before serving. The cake should be eaten on the day it is made.

To make more portions of this cake simply double or triple the above quantities and then cook each portion separately in individual mugs.

I love lemon drizzle cake – let's face it, who doesn't? So when in need of a quick fix this is the perfect cake to whip up. Filled with bursting blueberries and topped with a lemon drizzle this is a delicious cake to enjoy at any time of day. You can vary the berries if you wish – blackberries and raspberries also work well – and substitute the lemon with lime or orange. The possibilities are endless!

# LEMON AND BLUEBERRY CAKE

Place the butter in a heatproof bowl in the microwave and heat on full power for about 40 seconds until it has melted then leave it to cool.

Place the flour, sugar, milk, egg, melted butter and lemon zest in a mixing bowl and whisk together until everything is incorporated. Make sure that there are no lumps of flour. The batter should be thick and runny. Stir in the blueberries, reserving a few to sprinkle on the top.

Pour the batter into the mug until it is no more than three-quarters full. Do not overfill the mug otherwise it will overflow when cooking. Top with the remaining blueberries.

Cook on full power in a microwave (850W) for 3 minutes until the cake springs back to your touch. If you have a different power microwave, use the cooking time adjustment instructions on page 16.

When the cake is cooked make the lemon drizzle. Place the lemon juice and icing sugar in a separate bowl or mug and microwave on full power for 30 seconds, then whisk to ensure the icing sugar has dissolved and pour over the cake.

Serve warm straight away for best results. This cake needs to be eaten on the day it is made.

### HINTS AND TIPS

To make more portions of this cake simply double or triple the above quantities and then cook each portion separately in individual mugs.

I keep blueberries in my freezer and you can add them straight to the batter from frozen for equally tasty results. No need to defrost ahead and a year-round treat ready to hand!

SERVES: **1**
PREPARATION TIME: **5 minutes**
COOKING TIME: **3 minutes**
  **(850W microwave)**
EQUIPMENT: **1 microwave-**
  **proof mug (400ml/**
  **15fl oz/1½ cups), whisk**

45g/1½oz/2 tbsp butter
60g/2oz/3 tbsp self-raising/
  self-rising flour, sifted
60g/2oz/2 tbsp caster/
  superfine sugar
30ml/1fl oz/2 tbsp milk
20g/¾oz/1 tbsp beaten egg
Zest of 1 lemon
60g/2oz/2 tbsp fresh blueberries
For the lemon drizzle:
Juice of 1 lemon
30g/1oz/1 tbsp icing/
  confectioners' sugar

This is one indulgent little cake – gorgeously chocolately, topped with gooey marshmallow and chocolate chips. It is a perfect dessert to share with a loved one as it is rich and so probably one cup between two will do for a sweet treat. You can use any type of chocolate you like to add to the recipe so why not try orange chocolate, nutty chocolate or even chilli chocolate, if you are brave!

# CHOCOLATE CHIP MARSHMALLOW CAKE

**SERVES:** 1
**PREPARATION TIME:** 5 minutes
**COOKING TIME:** 3 minutes (850W microwave)
**EQUIPMENT:** 1 microwave-proof mug (400ml/ 15fl oz/1½ cups), whisk, baking parchment, piping/pastry bag, chef's blow torch (optional)

45g/1½oz/2 tbsp butter, plus extra for greasing
60g/2oz/3 tbsp self-raising/ self-rising flour, sifted
20g/⅔oz/1 tbsp cocoa powder, sifted, plus extra for dusting
60g/2oz/2 tbsp caster/ superfine sugar
30ml/1fl oz/2 tbsp milk
20g/¾oz/1 tbsp beaten egg
60g/2oz/2 tbsp milk, dark/ bittersweet or white chocolate chips (or a combination of any of these)
For the topping:
30ml/1fl oz/2 tbsp marshmallow fluff

Place the butter in a heatproof bowl in the microwave and heat on full power for about 40 seconds until it has melted then leave it to cool.

Place the flour, cocoa, sugar, milk, egg and melted butter in a mixing bowl and whisk together until everything is incorporated. Make sure that there are no lumps of flour. The batter should be thick. Stir in the chocolate chips.

Cut a piece of baking parchment into a rectangle about 2.5cm/1in taller than your mug and slightly wider than the circumference of your mug. Grease the mug with a little butter and place the baking parchment inside so that it lies flat around the sides of the mug with a little paper overlapping at the join. Pour the batter into the mug.

Pour the batter into the mug until it is no more than three-quarters full. Do not overfill the mug otherwise it will overflow when cooking.

Cook on full power in a microwave (850W) for 3 minutes until the cake springs back to your touch. If you have a different power microwave, use the cooking time adjustment instructions on page 16.

When the cake is cooked, remove the lining paper. Pipe the marshmallow fluff on top of the cake and, if you like, using a chef's blow torch, toast the outside of the marshmallow until it is lightly caramelized. Dust with cocoa powder and serve straight away for best results. This cake needs to be eaten on the day it is made.

## HINTS AND TIPS
If you do not have marshmallow fluff you can create a similar topping by using large marshmallows cut in half. Place on top of the finished cake and toast to caramelize. Marshmallow fluff is gluten- and dairy-free.

Red velvet cake is one of the most popular cakes in America – a vibrant dark red chocolate sponge topped with delicious cream cheese icing. You can decorate this cake with sugar sprinkles if you wish although I like the simplicity of a light dusting of cocoa powder.

# RED VELVET CAKE

SERVES: **1**
PREPARATION TIME: **5 minutes**
COOKING TIME: **3 minutes (850W microwave)**
EQUIPMENT: **1 microwave-proof mug (400ml/ 15fl oz/1½ cups), whisk, baking parchment, piping/pastry bag fitted with a small star nozzle**

45g/1½oz/2 tbsp butter, plus extra for greasing
60g/2oz/3 tbsp self-raising/ self-rising flour, sifted
20g/⅔oz/1 tbsp cocoa powder, sifted, plus extra for dusting
60g/2oz/2 tbsp caster/ superfine sugar
30ml/1fl oz/2 tbsp milk
20g/¾oz/1 tbsp beaten egg
5ml/1 tsp red food colouring
For the cream cheese frosting:
80g/2⅔oz/4 tbsp icing/ confectioners' sugar, sifted
20g/⅔oz/1 tbsp butter, softened
30g/1oz/1 tbsp cream cheese

Place the butter in a heatproof bowl in the microwave and heat on full power for about 40 seconds until it has melted then leave it to cool.

Place the flour, cocoa, sugar, milk, egg, melted butter and red food colouring in a mixing bowl and whisk together until everything is incorporated. Make sure that there are no lumps of flour. The batter should be thick and runny.

Cut a piece of baking parchment into a rectangle about 2.5cm/1in taller than your mug and slightly wider than the circumference of your mug. Grease the mug with a little butter and place the baking parchment inside so that it lies flat around the sides of the mug with a little paper overlapping at the join. Pour the batter into the mug.

Cook on full power in a microwave (850W) for 3 minutes until the cake springs back to your touch. If you have a different power microwave, use the cooking time adjustment instructions on page 16. Leave the cake to cool, then remove the lining paper.

For the icing, whisk together the icing sugar, butter and cream cheese until smooth and creamy. Spoon into the piping bag and pipe small star shapes on top of the cooled cake. Dust with cocoa to serve. This cake must be eaten on the day it is made.

## HINTS AND TIPS

Take care if you are making a gluten-free version of this cake (using the recipe on page 14) as some cocoa powders and icing/confectioners' sugars contain gluten.

Coffee and walnut cake is my Dad's favourite and this microwave version is perfect when you need a teatime treat topped with a coffee glacé icing and a whole walnut. To vary the cake you can replace the walnuts with other nuts such as pecans or brazil nuts for equally delicious results.

# COFFEE AND WALNUT CAKE

Place the butter in a heatproof bowl in the microwave and heat on full power for about 40 seconds until it has melted then leave it to cool.

Place the flour, sugar, milk, egg, melted butter and coffee extract in a mixing bowl and whisk together until everything is incorporated. Make sure that there are no lumps of flour. The batter should be thick and runny. Reserve one whole walnut half for decoration and then finely chop the rest using a sharp knife. Stir into the batter.

Cut a piece of baking parchment into a rectangle about 2.5cm/1in taller than your mug and slightly wider than the circumference of your mug. Grease the mug with a little butter and place the baking parchment inside so that it lies flat around the sides of the mug with a little paper overlapping at the join. Pour the batter into the mug.

Cook on full power in a microwave (850W) for 3 minutes until the cake springs back to your touch. If you have a different power microwave, use the cooking time adjustment instructions on page 16.

When the cake is cooked, place the icing sugar in a separate bowl and whisk in a few teaspoons of the dissolved coffee, adding gradually as you will not need it all, until the icing is smooth and thick. Remove the lining paper and pour the icing over the top of the cake and top with the reserved walnut half.

Serve straight away for best results. This cake needs to be eaten on the day it is made.

SERVES: 1
PREPARATION TIME: 5 minutes
COOKING TIME: 3 minutes
    (850W microwave)
EQUIPMENT: 1 microwave-
    proof mug (400ml/
    15fl oz/1½ cups), whisk,
    baking parchment

45g/1½oz/2 tbsp butter, plus
    extra for greasing
60g/2oz/3 tbsp self-raising/
    self-rising flour, sifted

60g/2oz/2 tbsp caster/
    superfine sugar
30ml/1fl oz/2 tbsp milk
20g/¾oz/1 tbsp beaten egg
5ml/1 tsp coffee extract
30g/1oz/2 tbsp walnut halves
For the icing:
45g/1½oz/2 tbsp icing/
    confectioners' sugar, sifted
5ml/1 tsp instant coffee
    granules dissolved in 15ml/
    1 tbsp of hot water

## HINTS AND TIPS
For an extra treat, you can melt a small amount of sugar in a pan until it caramelizes, and drizzle it over the reserved walnut half on a greased baking sheet to make a delicious praline nut topping for your cake.

Everyone loves carrot cake, but it can take quite a while to cook in the oven. This individual portion made in the microwave is ideal as it tastes just as delicious as regular carrot cake, yet can be made in a fraction of the time. Topped with classic cream cheese frosting and carrot decorations, it makes a perfect afternoon teatime treat (although personally I could eat this any time of the day!).

# CARROT CAKE

Place the butter in a heatproof bowl in the microwave and heat on full power for about 40 seconds until it has melted then leave it to cool.

Mix together the orange juice and zest, grated carrot and sultanas so that both the fruit and carrot are well coated in the juice. Add the ground cinnamon, ground ginger, milk, sugar, egg, melted butter and flour and whisk together until everything is incorporated. Make sure that there are no lumps of flour. The batter should be thick and runny.

Pour the batter into the mug until it is no more than three-quarters full. Do not overfill the mug otherwise it will overflow when cooking.

Cook on full power in a microwave (850W) for 3 minutes until the cake springs back to your touch. If you have a different power microwave, use the cooking time adjustment instructions on page 16.

When the cake is cooked, leave to cool whilst you make the icing. Whisk together the icing sugar, cream cheese, butter and orange juice until you have a smooth thick icing. Spread the icing over the top of the cake with a round-bladed knife. Decorate with the carrot decorations, if making an event of it, and a light dusting of cinnamon, if you like. This cake needs to be eaten on the day it is made.

## HINTS AND TIPS
If you have time to plan ahead you can make themed decorations! Make your own sugar carrots using ready-roll icing coloured orange and green with food colouring. To make lines on the carrots, press down lightly with a fork. Leave to dry overnight before using to decorate your cake.

SERVES: 1
PREPARATION TIME: 5 minutes
COOKING TIME: 3 minutes
(850W microwave)
EQUIPMENT: 1 microwave-
proof mug (400ml/
15fl oz/1½ cups), whisk

45g/1½oz/2 tbsp butter
Juice of ½ orange and 2.5ml/
½ tsp orange zest
30g/1oz/2 tbsp grated carrot
30g/1oz/1 tbsp sultanas/
golden raisins
2.5ml/½ tsp ground cinnamon
2.5ml/½ tsp ground ginger
30ml/1fl oz/2 tbsp milk
60g/2oz/2 tbsp caster/
superfine sugar
20g/¾oz/1 tbsp beaten egg
60g/2oz/3 tbsp self-raising/
self-rising flour, sifted
For the icing:
45g/1½oz/3 tbsp icing/
confectioners' sugar, sifted
15g/½oz/½ tbsp cream cheese
10ml/2 tsp butter, softened
5ml/1 tsp orange juice
sugar or chocolate carrots,
to decorate (optional)
cinnamon sugar, for dusting
(optional)

Rocky Road ice cream is one I remember well from my childhood – how can anyone resist the combination of chocolate, marshmallows and cherries? There are no real hard and fast rules about the ingredients for Rocky Road so you can go even further with added extras – a few chopped nuts would add a lovely crunchy texture, and I often add a spoon of marshmallow fluff.

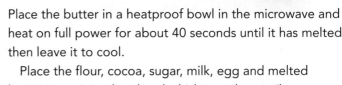

# ROCKY ROAD CAKE

SERVES: 1
PREPARATION TIME: 5 minutes
COOKING TIME: 3 minutes
   (850W microwave)
EQUIPMENT: 1 microwave-
   proof mug (400ml/
   15fl oz/1½ cups), whisk,
   baking parchment

45g/1½oz/2 tbsp butter, plus
   extra for greasing
60g/2oz/3 tbsp self-raising/
   self-rising flour, sifted
20g/⅔oz/1 tbsp cocoa
   powder, sifted
60g/2oz/2 tbsp caster/
   superfine sugar
30ml/1fl oz/2 tbsp milk
20g/¾oz/1 tbsp beaten egg
30g/1oz/1 tbsp glacé/
   candied cherries
15g/½oz/1 tbsp mini
   marshmallows
45g/1½oz/2 tbsp plain/semi-
   sweet chocolate, chopped

Place the butter in a heatproof bowl in the microwave and heat on full power for about 40 seconds until it has melted then leave it to cool.

Place the flour, cocoa, sugar, milk, egg and melted butter in a mixing bowl and whisk together until everything is incorporated. Finely chop the glacé cherries using a sharp knife. Fold in most of the cherries, marshmallows and chocolate, reserving some of each for decoration. Make sure that there are no lumps of flour. The batter should be thick and runny.

Cut a piece of baking parchment into a rectangle about 2.5cm/1in taller than your mug and slightly wider than the circumference of your mug. Grease the mug with a little butter and place the baking parchment inside so that it lies flat around the sides of the mug with a little paper overlapping at the join. Pour the batter into the mug.

Cook on full power in a microwave (850W) for 3 minutes until the cake springs back to your touch. If you have a different power microwave, use the cooking time adjustment instructions on page 16.

Remove the lining paper and sprinkle the top of the cake with the reserved chocolate, cherries and marshmallows. The warmth of the cake will melt the chocolate and soften the marshmallows. The cake should be eaten on the day it is made.

To make more portions of this cake simply double or triple the above quantities and then cook each portion separately in individual mugs.

# PUDDINGS

Warm steamed sponge puddings are such a treat but can take time to make. This chapter contains perfect miniature versions which can be ready in a matter of minutes, ideal for everyday suppers. With sticky toffee, pineapple upside down and molten lava puddings, you will be spoilt for choice.

Tucking into pineapple upside down pudding is one of my childhood memories – I remember this cake being made for us when we were little and being amazed that what looked like a very plain cake from the outside, when inverted became a glistening delight topped with rings of pineapple and kitsch glacé cherries. You can make individual portions of this pudding so easily in the microwave that it makes a perfect last-minute dessert.

# PINEAPPLE UPSIDE DOWN PUDDING

Place the butter in a heatproof bowl in the microwave and heat on full power for about 40 seconds until it has melted then leave it to cool.

Place the flour, ground almonds, sugar, milk, egg, melted butter and vanilla in a mixing bowl and whisk together until everything is incorporated. Make sure that there are no lumps of flour. The batter should be thick and runny.

Cut a piece of baking parchment into a rectangle about 2.5cm/1in taller than your mug and slightly wider than the circumference of your mug. Grease the mug with a little butter and place the baking parchment inside so that it lies flat around the sides of the mug with a little paper overlapping at the join.

Place a spoonful of golden syrup in the bottom of the mug and press the pineapple ring into the syrup. Depending on the size of your mug you may need to cut the ring so that it fits. Pop the cherry into the hole in the pineapple ring then pour the batter into the mug until it is no more than three-quarters full.

Cook on full power in a microwave (850W) for 3 minutes until the cake springs back to your touch. If you have a different power microwave, use the cooking time adjustment instructions on page 16.

Leave the cake to cool for a minute, then slide a knife around the edge of the mug and invert the mug into a bowl. Remove the lining paper. Place the remaining golden syrup in a second mug or bowl with 15ml/1 tbsp of water and microwave on full power for 30 seconds. Pour the hot golden syrup over the pudding and serve straight away with custard.

This cake is best eaten on the day it is made. To make more portions of this cake simply double or triple the above quantities and then cook each portion separately.

SERVES: **1**
PREPARATION TIME: **5 minutes**
COOKING TIME: **3 minutes** (850W microwave)
EQUIPMENT: **1 microwave-proof mug (400ml/ 15fl oz/1½ cups), whisk, baking parchment**

45g/1½oz/2 tbsp butter, plus extra for greasing
40g/1⅓oz/2 tbsp self-raising/ self-rising flour, sifted
30g/1oz/1 tbsp ground almonds
60g/2oz/2 tbsp caster/ superfine sugar
30ml/1fl oz/2 tbsp milk
20g/¾oz/1 tbsp beaten egg
5ml/1 tsp vanilla bean paste or vanilla extract
30ml/1fl oz/2 tbsp golden/ light corn syrup
1 pineapple ring
1 glacé/candied cherry
Custard, to serve, see below

### HINTS AND TIPS

To make a quick custard in the microwave, mix 15ml/1 tbsp custard powder and 10ml/2 tsp caster/ superfine sugar with 250ml/8fl oz/1 cup milk, mixing in gradually so the custard powder is all blended in. Microwave on full power for about 2½ minutes, whisking every minute.

Sticky toffee pudding in always a winner – a buttery toffee sponge studded with dates and served with a rich and indulgent sauce that tastes like warm amber nectar. You can serve this delicious pudding with cream or custard for an extra-special treat.

# STICKY TOFFEE PUDDING

**SERVES: 1**
**PREPARATION TIME: 5 minutes**
**COOKING TIME: 3 minutes (850W microwave)**
**EQUIPMENT: 1 microwave-proof mug (400ml/ 15fl oz/1½ cups), whisk, baking parchment**

45g/1½oz/2 tbsp butter, plus extra for greasing
40g/1⅓oz/2 tbsp self-raising/ self-rising flour, sifted
30g/1oz/1 tbsp ground almonds
60g/2oz/2 tbsp muscovado/ molasses or soft dark brown sugar
3 stoned/pitted dates, finely chopped
5ml/1 tsp vanilla extract
30ml/1fl oz/2 tbsp milk
20g/¾oz/1 tbsp beaten egg

For the sauce:
30g/1oz/1tbsp muscovado/ molasses or soft dark brown sugar
30g/1oz/1 tbsp caster/ superfine sugar
45g/1½ oz/2 tbsp butter
60ml/4 tbsp double/ heavy cream

Begin by making the sauce. Place the muscovado and caster sugar, butter and cream in a microwaveproof bowl and microwave on full power (850W) for 1 minute then remove from the microwave and stir well. Return to the microwave and cook for a further minute on full power. Remove from the microwave carefully as the sauce will be hot, stir well and set aside.

Place the butter in a heatproof bowl in the microwave and heat on full power for about 40 seconds until it has melted then leave it to cool.

Place the flour, ground almonds, sugar, dates, vanilla, milk, egg and melted butter in a mixing bowl and whisk together until everything is incorporated. Make sure that there are no lumps of flour. The batter should be thick and runny.

Cut a piece of baking parchment into a rectangle about 2.5cm/1in taller than your mug and slightly wider than the circumference of your mug. Grease the mug with a little butter and place the baking parchment inside so that it lies flat around the sides of the mug with a little paper overlapping at the join.

Pour the batter into the mug and cook on full power in a microwave (850W) for 3 minutes until the cake springs back to your touch. If you have a different power microwave, use the cooking time adjustment instructions on page 16.

Leave the cake to cool for a minute, then remove the lining paper and slide a knife around the edge of the mug and invert the cake into a bowl. Pour over the sauce to serve. This cake must be eaten on the day it is made.

To make more portions of this cake simply double or triple the above quantities and then cook each portion separately in individual mugs.

These little sponges remind me of school – it was always a good day when there was jam pudding on the lunch menu. These puddings are so versatile as you can make them with any flavour of jam. Fruit curds also work brilliantly or why not try a few tablespoons of maple or golden syrup for syrup sponges. These make great puddings for hungry kids after a busy day at school!

# SPONGE PUDDING WITH JAM, SYRUP OR LEMON CURD

Place the butter in a heatproof bowl in the microwave and heat on full power for about 40 seconds until it has melted then leave it to cool.

Place the flour, ground almonds, sugar, milk, egg, melted butter and vanilla in a mixing bowl and whisk together until everything is incorporated. Make sure that there are no lumps of flour. The batter should be thick and runny.

Cut a piece of baking parchment into a rectangle about 2.5cm/1in taller than your mug and slightly wider than the circumference of your mug. Grease the mug with a little butter and place the baking parchment inside so that it lies flat around the sides of the mug with a little paper overlapping at the join.

Spoon the jam, golden syrup or lemon curd into the bottom of the mug and pour over the batter.

Cook on full power in a microwave (850W) for 3 minutes until the cake springs back to your touch. If you have a different power microwave, use the cooking time adjustment instructions on page 16.

Leave the cake to cool for a minute, then slide a knife around the edge of the mug and remove the lining paper. Invert the cake into a bowl so that the jam, syrup or lemon curd is on top.

This cake is best eaten warm and should be eaten on the day it is made.

SERVES: 1
PREPARATION TIME: 5 minutes
COOKING TIME: 3 minutes
  (850W microwave)
EQUIPMENT: 1 microwave
  proof mug (400ml/
  15fl oz/1½ cups), whisk,
  baking parchment

45g/1½oz/2 tbsp butter, plus
  extra for greasing
40g/1⅓oz/2 tbsp self-raising/
  self-rising flour, sifted
30g/1oz/1 tbsp ground almonds
60g/2oz/2 tbsp caster/
  superfine sugar
30ml/1fl oz/2 tbsp milk
20g/¾oz/1 tbsp beaten egg
5ml/1 tsp vanilla bean paste or
  vanilla extract
30ml/1fl oz/2 tbsp strawberry
  jam, golden/light corn syrup
  or lemon curd

**HINTS AND TIPS**
You can add fresh fruit or sultanas/golden raisins to the batter for an extra treat.

To make a lower fat version use sugar-free or reduced sugar jam and low-fat baking spread.

I love ginger a lot! Ginger beer, ginger cake, ginger tea – you name it, if it has ginger in it, I love it! This is therefore one of my favourite puddings to whisk up if I need a warming treat after work. The sponge is flavoured with ground ginger and stem ginger and is topped with a delicious lemon curd icing – lemon and ginger are a match made in heaven.

# GINGER SPONGE CAKE

Place the butter in a heatproof bowl in the microwave and heat on full power for about 40 seconds until it has melted then leave it to cool.

Place the flour, sugar, milk, egg, melted butter, ground ginger and stem ginger in a mixing bowl and whisk together until everything is incorporated. You can do this in the mug itself if you prefer. Make sure that there are no lumps of flour. The batter should be thick and runny.

Pour the batter into the mug until it is no more than three-quarters full. Do not overfill the mug otherwise it will overflow when cooking.

Cook on full power in a microwave (850W) for 3 minutes until the cake springs back to your touch. If you have a different power microwave, use the cooking time adjustment instructions on page 16. Whilst the cake is still warm pour the ginger syrup over the top to glaze the cake.

Allow the cake to cool. To prepare the icing, whisk together the icing sugar, lemon curd and water (you may not need all the water so add gradually) to make a smooth icing, then spread over the cake. Decorate with the crystallized ginger. The cake should be eaten on the day it is made.

**SERVES: 1**
**PREPARATION TIME: 5 minutes**
**COOKING TIME: 3 minutes**
  **(850W microwave)**
**EQUIPMENT: 1 microwave-**
  **proof mug (400ml/**
  **15fl oz/1½ cups), whisk**

45g/1½oz/2 tbsp butter
60g/2oz/3 tbsp self-raising/
  self-rising flour, sifted
60g/2oz/2 tbsp caster/
  superfine sugar
30ml/1fl oz/2 tbsp milk
20g/¾oz/1 tbsp beaten egg
2.5ml/½ tsp ground ginger
30g/1oz/1 tbsp finely chopped
  stem ginger in syrup plus
  15ml/1 tbsp of the syrup
To decorate:
60g/2oz/2 tbsp icing/
  confectioners' sugar, sifted
5–10ml/1–2 tsp lemon curd
5–10ml/1–2 tsp water
Small pieces of crystallized
  ginger

### HINTS AND TIPS
If you are making a lactose-/dairy-free version of this cake, following the recipe on page 15, decorate with a lemon icing by mixing 60g/2oz/2 tbsp of sifted icing sugar with 5–10ml/1–2 tsp fresh lemon juice and topping with the crystallized ginger, as lemon curd contains dairy products.

This is a great cake to make when plums are ripe in the summer season, and when it is inverted, the glistening red plums appear surrounded by a light cinnamon sponge. You can also make this cake with slices of fresh nectarines, peaches, or even greengages if you are lucky enough to find them. It is important that the plums you use are ripe and juicy.

# UPSIDE DOWN PLUM CAKE

Place the butter in a heatproof bowl in the microwave and heat on full power for about 40 seconds until it has melted then leave it to cool.

Cut a piece of baking parchment into a rectangle about 2.5cm/1in taller than your mug and slightly wider than the circumference of your mug. Grease the mug with a little butter and place the baking parchment inside so that it lies flat around the sides of the mug with a little paper overlapping at the join.

Place the plum quarters in the bottom of the mug and sprinkle with the sugar and ground cinnamon.

Place the flour, sugar, milk, egg, melted butter and ground cinnamon in a mixing bowl and whisk together until everything is incorporated. Make sure that there are no lumps of flour. The batter should be thick and runny. Pour the batter into the mug over the plums.

Cook on full power in a microwave (850W) for 3 minutes until the cake springs back to your touch. If you have a different power microwave, use the cooking time adjustment instructions on page 16.

When the cake is cooked, remove the lining paper and invert the cake into a bowl to serve so that the plums are visible on top. Serve warm for best results, with custard if you wish.

## HINTS AND TIPS
This cake is yummy served with a cinnamon custard. To make this use 15ml/1 tbsp custard powder, 10ml/ 2 tsp caster/superfine sugar and 2.5ml/½ tsp ground cinnamon and mix with 250ml/8fl oz/1 cup milk, adding the milk gradually so it is well blended. Microwave on full power for 2½ minutes, whisking after each minute.

SERVES: 1
PREPARATION TIME: 5 minutes
COOKING TIME: 3 minutes
(850W microwave)
EQUIPMENT: 1 microwave-
proof mug (400ml/
15fl oz/1½ cups), whisk,
baking parchment

75g/2½oz/1½ ripe plums,
stones/pits removed and cut
into quarters
30g/1oz/1 tbsp caster/
superfine sugar
2.5ml/½ tsp ground cinnamon
45g/1½oz/2 tbsp butter, plus
extra for greasing
60g/2oz/3 tbsp self-raising/
self-rising flour, sifted
60g/2oz/2 tbsp caster/
superfine sugar
30ml/1fl oz/2 tbsp milk
20g/¾oz/1 tbsp beaten egg
2.5ml/½ tsp ground cinnamon
Custard, to serve (optional),
see hints and tips

This super-easy cake has a delicious molten chocolate centre. My version is made with orange chocolate and orange zest but you can vary the flavour easily, if you prefer – why not try a chocolate mint version or even use a chilli-spiced chocolate for a fiery kick?

# MOLTEN LAVA CHOC

SERVES: 1
PREPARATION TIME: 5 minutes
COOKING TIME: 3 minutes
(850W microwave)
EQUIPMENT: 1 microwave-
proof mug (400ml/
15fl oz/1½ cups), whisk,
baking parchment

45g/1½oz/2 tbsp butter, plus
extra for greasing
60g/2oz/3 tbsp self-raising/
self-rising flour, sifted
30g/1oz/1 tbsp cocoa powder,
sifted, plus extra for dusting
60g/2oz/2 tbsp caster/
superfine sugar
30ml/1fl oz/2 tbsp milk
20g/¾oz/1 tbsp beaten egg
2.5ml/½ tsp orange zest
60g/2oz/2 tbsp plain/semi-
sweet orange-flavoured
chocolate, in large chunks

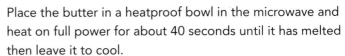

Place the butter in a heatproof bowl in the microwave and heat on full power for about 40 seconds until it has melted then leave it to cool.

Place the flour, cocoa, sugar, milk, egg, melted butter and orange zest in a mixing bowl and whisk together until everything is incorporated. Make sure that there are no lumps of flour. The batter should be thick and runny.

Cut a piece of baking parchment into a rectangle about 2.5cm/1in taller than your mug and slightly wider than the circumference of your mug. Grease the mug with a little butter and place the baking parchment inside so that it lies flat around the sides of the mug with a little paper overlapping at the join. Pour the batter into the mug. Press the chunks of chocolate into the centre of the cake so that they are just below the surface.

Cook on full power in a microwave (850W) for 3 minutes until the cake springs back to your touch. If you have a different power microwave, use the cooking time adjustment instructions on page 16.

When the cake is cooked, remove the baking parchment and dust the top of the cake liberally with cocoa powder. Serve the cake warm. This cake must be eaten on the day it is made.

To make more portions of this cake simply double or triple the above quantities and then cook each portion separately in individual mugs.

### HINTS AND TIPS
For a delectable chocolate cherry version, add a few pitted fresh cherries with plain/semisweet chocolate chunks into the centre of the cake and omit the orange zest.

A traditional baked Alaska is such a treat with chilly ice cream and hot toasted meringue. Classically it is made with Italian meringue – egg whites cooked with hot sugar syrup. Making this takes some time so this is my quick cheat's microwave version using soft meringue or – even easier – using ready-made marshmallow fluff. Toasted and caramelized with a blow torch, this is a perfect last-minute dessert!

# BAKED ALASKA

Place the butter in a heatproof bowl in the microwave and heat on full power for about 40 seconds until it has melted then leave it to cool.

Place the flour, cocoa, sugar, milk, egg and melted butter in a mixing bowl and whisk together until everything is incorporated. Make sure that there are no lumps of flour. The batter should be thick and runny.

Cut a piece of baking parchment into a rectangle about 2.5cm/1in taller than your mug and slightly wider than the circumference of your mug. Grease the mug with a little butter and place the baking parchment inside so that it lies flat around the sides of the mug with a little paper overlapping at the join. Pour the batter into the mug until it is no more than three-quarters full.

Cook on full power in a microwave (850W) for 3 minutes until the cake springs back to your touch. If you have a different power microwave, use the cooking time adjustment instructions on page 16. Leave to cool completely then remove from the mug, remove the lining paper and cut in half horizontally so that you have two even sized round discs of cake.

If making your own meringue, whisk the egg whites with a pinch of salt to soft peaks, then add the sugar 15ml/ 1 tbsp at a time until the meringue is thick and glossy.

You need to work quickly when you are ready to serve so that the ice cream does not melt. Place each disc of cake on a serving plate and top with a scoop of ice cream. Using a round-bladed knife spread a thick layer of meringue or marshmallow fluff over the cake and ice cream. Toast the outside of the meringue or marshmallow fluff with a blow torch until caramelized and serve immediately.

SERVES: **1**
PREPARATION TIME: **10 minutes**
COOKING TIME: **3 minutes (850W microwave)**
EQUIPMENT: **1 microwave-proof mug (400ml/ 15fl oz/1½ cups), whisk, baking parchment, chef's blow torch**

45g/1½oz/2 tbsp butter, plus extra for greasing

60g/2oz/3 tbsp self-raising/ self-rising flour, sifted
20g/⅔oz/1 tbsp cocoa powder, sifted
60g/2oz/2 tbsp caster/ superfine sugar
30ml/1fl oz/2 tbsp milk
20g/¾oz/1 tbsp beaten egg
For the filling and topping:
1 egg white, a pinch of salt and 50g/2oz/¼ cup caster/ superfine sugar or 75g/3oz/ ¾ cup marshmallow fluff
1 scoop of ice cream, flavour of your choosing

## HINTS AND TIPS
If you are making the meringue, it does contain raw egg and so is not suitable for pregnant women or very young children.

# FRUITY CUPS

The recipes in this chapter are bursting with all your favourite fruits – raspberries, bananas and apples, to name but a few. For an impressive dessert for entertaining why not try the chocolate-stuffed pear nestled in a rich chocolate sponge or for an afternoon tea treat, the strawberry layer cake is the perfect three-minute replacement for a Victoria sponge.

Banana and walnut cakes are always popular and this quick and easy microwave version is no exception – moist from the bananas and topped with a fun yellow icing and salty pretzels, it makes a great cake to serve for friends. Make sure that you use a really ripe banana for best results – I usually leave mine in the fruit bowl until it has large black spots!

# BANANA AND WALNUT PRETZEL CAKE

Place the butter in a heatproof bowl in the microwave and heat on full power for about 40 seconds until it has melted then leave it to cool.

Blitz the walnuts to fine pieces in a food processor. Mash the banana in a bowl with a fork to a smooth purée then fold in most of the walnut crumbs, reserving a few for decoration.

Place the flour, sugar, milk, egg, melted butter and banana mixture in a mixing bowl and whisk together until everything is incorporated. Make sure that there are no lumps of flour. The batter should be thick and runny.

Pour the batter into the mug until it is no more than two thirds full. Do not overfill the mug otherwise it may overflow when cooking.

Cook on full power in a microwave (850W) for 3 minutes until the cake springs back to your touch. If you have a different power microwave, use the cooking time adjustment instructions on page 16.

When the cake is cooked, place the icing sugar, food colouring and a little water in a separate bowl and stir until you have a thick icing. Spoon over the cooled cake, sprinkle with the reserved blitzed walnuts and top with a pretzel for decoration. This cake must be eaten on the day it is made.

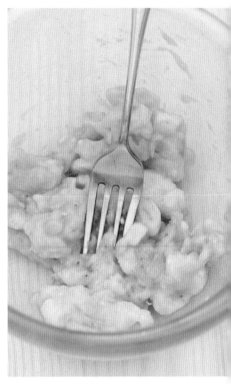

SERVES: **1**
PREPARATION TIME: **5 minutes**
COOKING TIME: **3 minutes
(850W microwave)**
EQUIPMENT: **1 microwave-
proof mug (400ml/
15fl oz/1½ cups),
whisk, blender**

45g/1½oz/2 tbsp butter
30g/1oz/1 tbsp walnut pieces
½ ripe banana
60g/2oz/3 tbsp self-raising/
    self-rising flour, sifted
60g/2oz/2 tbsp caster/
    superfine sugar
30ml/1fl oz/2 tbsp milk
20g/¾oz/1 tbsp beaten egg

For the icing:
30g/1oz/1 tbsp icing/
    confectioners' sugar, sifted
A few drops of yellow
    food colouring
5–10ml/1–2 tsp water
1 small salted pretzel

## HINTS AND TIPS
To make gluten-free or dairy-/lactose-free versions of this cake, use the basic batters on pages 14 and 15, adding the same quantities of banana and walnuts as listed. Make the icing in the same way, making sure that the icing/confectioners' sugar is gluten-free and that you use gluten- and dairy-free pretzels.

Fresh apples on sticks dipped in caramel are a classic autumn treat – perfect for Halloween and Bonfire Parties. This little cake takes inspiration from the humble toffee apple and is quick and easy to prepare. Filled with fresh apple and topped with salted caramel sauce, it is a cake that you will just want to dig into with a big spoon.

# TOFFEE APPLE CAKE

SERVES: 1

PREPARATION TIME: **5 minutes**

COOKING TIME: **3 minutes**
(850W microwave)

EQUIPMENT: **1 microwave-proof mug (400ml/ 15fl oz/1½ cups), whisk, baking parchment**

1 small apple (approx 75g/ 2½oz), peeled and cored

45g/1½oz/2 tbsp butter, plus extra for greasing

60g/2oz/3 tbsp self-raising/ self-rising flour, sifted

60g/2oz/2 tbsp caster/ superfine sugar

5ml/1 tsp ground cinnamon

30ml/1fl oz/2 tbsp milk

20g/¾oz/1 tbsp beaten egg

30ml/1fl oz/2 tbsp store-bought salted caramel sauce

Caramel chocolate curls, to decorate (optional)

Chop the peeled apple into approximately 2cm/¾in pieces and place in a heatproof bowl with 30ml/1fl oz/ 2 tbsp of water. Microwave on full power for 1 minute until the apple is just starting to go soft. Strain the apple to remove the water and set aside to cool whilst you make the cake batter.

Place the butter in a second heatproof bowl in the microwave and heat on full power for about 40 seconds until it has melted then leave it to cool.

Place the flour, sugar, cinnamon, milk, egg and melted butter in a mixing bowl and whisk together until everything is incorporated. Make sure that there are no lumps of flour. The batter should be thick and runny. Fold in the cooked apple.

Cut a piece of baking parchment into a rectangle about 2.5cm/1in taller than your mug and slightly wider than the circumference of your mug. Grease the mug with a little butter and place the baking parchment inside so that it lies flat around the sides of the mug with a little paper overlapping at the join. Pour half of the batter into the mug and place a spoonful of the caramel sauce on top, then cover with more batter.

Cook on full power in a microwave (850W) for 3 minutes until the cake springs back to your touch. If you have a different power microwave, use the cooking time adjustment instructions on page 16.

Top the cake with the second spoonful of caramel sauce whilst it is still hot so that it melts over the top of the cake. For extra decoration you can add caramel chocolate curls. Remove the lining paper and serve warm for best results. This cake must be eaten on the day it is made.

## HINTS AND TIPS

Salted caramel sauce is now widely available in supermarkets, but if you cannot find any replace with regular toffee sauce instead, adding a small pinch of salt, and it will taste just as good. Alternatively you can make your own thin salted caramel sauce, following the recipe on p85.

Pear and chocolate are one of those wonderful combinations that can't fail to delight. This recipe is no exception – a juicy pear filled with chocolate and surrounded by a rich chocolate sponge. The pear poking out of the cake makes a wonderful centrepiece with no other decoration needed.

# PEAR AND CHOCOLATE CAKE

Place the butter in a heatproof bowl in the microwave and heat on full power for about 40 seconds until it has melted then leave it to cool.

Place the flour, cocoa, sugar, milk, egg and melted butter in a mixing bowl and whisk together until everything is incorporated. Make sure that there are no lumps of flour. The batter should be thick and runny.

Using a swivel peeler or sharp knife, peel the skin from the pear, taking care to leave the stem intact. Using the melon baller, scoop out the core of the pear from the bottom of the fruit so that the pear remains intact and it has an empty cavity inside where the core was. Place the squares of chocolate inside the cavity. Do not do this in advance of cooking otherwise the pear will brown although you can prevent this if you cover in a little lemon juice.

Grease and line the mug following the instructions on page 19. Pour the batter into the mug until it is no more than half full and place the pear into the sponge batter. Do not overfill the mug otherwise it will overflow when cooking. You may not need all of the batter but it is not possible to make it in a smaller quantity.

Cook on full power in a microwave (850W) for 3 minutes until the cake springs back to your touch. If you have a different power microwave, use the cooking time adjustment instructions on page 16.

Leave the cake for a minute to cool then remove the lining paper and serve straight away warm for best results. The cake should be eaten on the day it is made.

SERVES: 1
PREPARATION TIME: 5 minutes
COOKING TIME: 3 minutes
   (850W microwave)
EQUIPMENT: swivel peeler, melon baller, whisk, 1 microwaveproof mug (400ml/15fl oz/1½ cups), baking parchment

45g/1½oz/2 tbsp butter, plus extra for greasing

60g/2oz/3 tbsp self-raising/self-rising flour, sifted
20g/⅔oz/1 tbsp cocoa powder, sifted
60g/2oz/2 tbsp caster/superfine sugar
30ml/1fl oz/2 tbsp milk
20g/¾oz/1 tbsp beaten egg
1 small ripe pear
15g/½oz/½ tbsp plain/semi-sweet chocolate squares

This cake is positively festive, bursting with a compôte of clementines and cranberries at the bottom of the cake. If you wish you can invert the cake into a bowl from the mug so that the delicious fruit is on the top. The sponge is delicately flavoured with clementine zest but you can replace with satsuma or orange zest and segments, if clementines are not available.

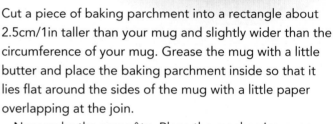

# CRANBERRY AND CLEMENTINE CAKE

SERVES: **1**
PREPARATION TIME: **5 minutes**
COOKING TIME: **3 minutes**
   **(850W microwave)**
EQUIPMENT: **1 microwave-proof mug (400ml/15fl oz/1½ cups), whisk, baking parchment**

45g/1½oz/2 tbsp butter, plus extra for greasing
60g/2oz/3 tbsp self-raising/self-rising flour, sifted
60g/2oz/2 tbsp caster/superfine sugar
30ml/1fl oz/2 tbsp milk
20g/¾oz/1 tbsp beaten egg
2.5ml/½ tsp clementine zest
For the fruit compôte:
28g/1oz/1½ tbsp fresh cranberries
30g/1oz/1 tbsp caster/superfine sugar
1 clementine, peeled and any seeds removed

Cut a piece of baking parchment into a rectangle about 2.5cm/1in taller than your mug and slightly wider than the circumference of your mug. Grease the mug with a little butter and place the baking parchment inside so that it lies flat around the sides of the mug with a little paper overlapping at the join.

Now make the compôte. Place the cranberries, sugar and clementine segments in a microwaveproof bowl and heat on full power for 1 minute until the fruit is soft. Stir half way through cooking. Spoon the fruit mixture into the bottom of the lined mug.

Place the butter in a heatproof bowl in the microwave and heat on full power for about 40 seconds until it has melted then leave it to cool.

Place the flour, sugar, milk, egg, melted butter and clementine zest in a mixing bowl and whisk together until everything is incorporated. Make sure that there are no lumps of flour. The batter should be thick and runny.

Pour the batter into the mug on top of the fruit compôte. Cook on full power in a microwave (850W) for 3 minutes until the cake springs back to your touch. If you have a different power microwave, use the cooking time adjustment instructions on page 16.

When the cake is cooked, remove the lining paper and invert the cake into a bowl so that the fruit compôte is on top. Leave to cool for a minute and then serve.

**HINTS AND TIPS**
Fresh cranberries can be frozen and you can use them straight from the freezer in this recipe. If you cannot find fresh cranberries, you can use dried cranberries in their place.

This little cake is bursting with berries and has a heady hint of almond. It is delicious served with a large spoonful of cream. My preference is to serve this with clotted cream and a few extra berries but whipped cream works well too. This recipe is very versatile and you can easily substitute other fresh berries in place of the raspberries – blackberries, blueberries or even strawberries all work well.

# RASPBERRY AND ALMOND CREAM CAKE

Place the butter in a heatproof bowl in the microwave and heat on full power for about 40 seconds until it has melted then leave it to cool.

Place the flour, ground almonds, sugar, milk, egg, melted butter and almond extract in a mixing bowl and whisk together until everything is incorporated. Make sure that there are no lumps of flour. The batter should be thick and runny. Stir in the fresh raspberries reserving a few to serve on top of the cake after it is cooked.

Grease and line the mug following the instructions on page 19. Pour the batter into the mug until it is no more than three-quarters full. Do not overfill the mug otherwise it will overflow when cooking.

Cook on full power in a microwave (850W) for 3 minutes until the cake springs back to your touch. If you have a different power microwave, use the cooking time adjustment instructions on page 16.

When the cake is cooked, leave to cool and then remove the lining paper and top with a spoonful of cream and the reserved fresh raspberries and freeze-dried raspberries. This cake is best eaten on the day it is made.

SERVES: 1
PREPARATION TIME: 5 minutes
COOKING TIME: 3 minutes
  (850W microwave)
EQUIPMENT: 1 microwave-
  proof mug (400ml/
  15fl oz/1½ cups), whisk,
  baking parchment

45g/1½oz/2 tbsp butter, plus
  extra for greasing
40g/1⅓oz/2 tbsp self-raising/
  self-rising flour, sifted

30g/1oz/1 tbsp ground
  almonds
60g/2oz/2 tbsp caster/
  superfine sugar
30ml/1fl oz/2 tbsp milk
20g/¾oz/1 tbsp beaten egg
5ml/1 tsp almond extract
70g/2½oz/2 tbsp fresh
  raspberries
5ml/1 tsp freeze-dried
  raspberries, chopped
Clotted cream or whipped
  cream, to serve

## HINTS AND TIPS
If you want to make a raspberry sauce to serve with the cake, crush 100g/3¾oz/3 tbsp raspberries with 30g/1oz/1 tbsp icing/confectioners' sugar to release all the juice. Pass the mixture through a sieve or strainer to remove the seeds and then drizzle over the cake.

Ripe cherries are perfect in cakes and this quick and easy version is no exception. If you cannot get fresh cherries you can use preserved cherries instead or if you have cherry compôte, place a spoonful into the bottom of your mug and pour the batter on top for a cherry surprise cake.

# CHERRY AND VANILLA SPONGE CAKE

**SERVES:** 1
**PREPARATION TIME:** 5 minutes
**COOKING TIME:** 3 minutes
  (850W microwave)
**EQUIPMENT:** 1 microwave-
  proof mug (400ml/
  15fl oz/1½ cups),
  whisk, cherry pitter,
  baking parchment

45g/1½oz/2 tbsp butter, plus
  extra for greasing
60g/2oz/3 tbsp self-raising/
  self-rising flour, sifted
60g/2oz/2 tbsp caster/
  superfine sugar
30ml/1fl oz/2 tbsp milk
20g/¾oz/1 tbsp beaten egg
5ml/1 tsp vanilla extract
100g/3¾oz/generous
  ½ cup fresh cherries
15g/½oz/½ tbsp caster/
  superfine sugar
For the topping:
50ml/2fl oz/¼ cup double/
  heavy cream, whipped
1 fresh whole cherry

Place the butter in a heatproof bowl in the microwave and heat on full power for about 40 seconds until it has melted then leave it to cool.

Place the flour, sugar, milk, egg, melted butter and vanilla in a mixing bowl and whisk together until everything is incorporated. Make sure that there are no lumps of flour. The batter should be thick and runny.

Remove the pits from the cherries using the cherry pitter (remove any stalks as well). If you do not have a cherry pitter, cut the cherries in half and remove the pits that way. Place the pitted cherries in a bowl with the caster sugar and stir.

Cut a piece of baking parchment into a rectangle about 2.5cm/1in taller than your mug and slightly wider than the circumference of your mug. Grease the mug with a little butter and place the baking parchment inside so that it lies flat around the sides of the mug with a little paper overlapping at the join.

Pour the batter into the mug. Pile the cake batter high with the sugar-coated cherries (they will sink into the batter during cooking).

Cook on full power in a microwave (850W) for 3 minutes until the cake springs back to your touch. If you have a different power microwave, use the cooking time adjustment instructions on page 16.

Allow the cake to cool before removing the lining paper and adding the whipped cream and topping with a fresh cherry. The cake should be eaten on the day it is made.

To make more portions of this cake simply double or triple the above quantities and then cook each portion separately in individual mugs.

Nothing beats a Victoria sandwich cake – vanilla sponge cake layers sandwiched with buttercream or fresh cream and jam. This is my easy peasy mini microwave version for when you want to sit in the garden in the summer and indulge but don't have time to bake.

# STRAWBERRY LAYER CAKE

Place the butter in a heatproof bowl in the microwave and heat on full power for about 40 seconds until it has melted then leave it to cool.

Place the flour, sugar, milk, egg, melted butter and vanilla in a mixing bowl and whisk together until everything is incorporated. Make sure that there are no lumps of flour. The batter should be thick and runny.

Cut a piece of baking parchment into a rectangle about 2.5cm/1in taller than your mug and slightly wider than the circumference of your mug. Grease the mug with a little butter and place the baking parchment inside so that it lies flat around the sides of the mug with a little paper overlapping at the join.

Pour the batter into the mug and cook on full power in a microwave (850W) for 3 minutes until the cake springs back to your touch. If you have a different power microwave, use the cooking time adjustment instructions on page 16.

When the cake is cooked, leave to cool and then remove the lining paper. Slide a knife around the side of the cake and remove from the mug. Using a sharp knife cut the cake into three equal horizontal layers. Place one disc of cake on a serving plate and top with cream and a little jam. Finely slice the strawberries and place half on top of the cream. Top with a second layer of cake and place a little more cream and jam and some strawberry slices on top and then finish with the top layer of cake. Dust with icing sugar to serve. The cake should be eaten on the day it is made.

To make more portions of this cake simply double or triple the above quantities and then cook each portion separately in individual mugs.

SERVES: **1**
PREPARATION TIME: **5 minutes**
COOKING TIME: **3 minutes**
   **(850W microwave)**
EQUIPMENT: **1 straight-sided microwaveproof mug (400ml/15fl oz/1½ cups), whisk, baking parchment**

45g/1½oz/2 tbsp butter, plus extra for greasing
60g/2oz/3 tbsp self-raising/ self-rising flour, sifted
60g/2oz/2 tbsp caster/ superfine sugar
30ml/1fl oz/2 tbsp milk
20g/¾oz/1 tbsp beaten egg
5ml/1 tsp vanilla extract
To assemble:
30ml/2 tbsp clotted cream or 60ml/4 tbsp double/ heavy cream, whipped to stiff peaks
15ml/1 tbsp strawberry jam
2 large strawberries, hulled
Icing/confectioners' sugar, for dusting

# FANCY CUPS

This chapter contains indulgent cups filled with boozy grown-up treats and rich puddings. They are perfectly suited for when the kids have gone to bed. Why not try an Irish cream liqueur cake curled up in front of the fire or a whisky and marmalade syrup cake.

This cake is ideal for those who love gin and tonic – a lovely light lemon cake with a gin and lemon drizzle poured over. If you like lime with gin you can substitute the lemon for lime juice and zest if you prefer – I love both types of cake equally!

# GIN AND LEMON DRIZZLE CAKE

Place the butter in a heatproof bowl in the microwave and heat on full power for about 40 seconds until it has melted then leave it to cool.

Place the flour, sugar, milk, egg, melted butter and lemon zest in a mixing bowl and whisk together until everything is incorporated. Make sure that there are no lumps of flour. The batter should be thick and runny.

Cut a piece of baking parchment into a rectangle about 2.5cm/1in taller than your mug and slightly wider than the circumference of your mug. Grease the mug with a little butter and place the baking parchment inside so that it lies flat around the sides of the mug with a little paper overlapping at the join. Pour the batter into the mug.

Cook on full power in a microwave (850W) for 3 minutes until the cake springs back to your touch. If you have a different power microwave, use the cooking time adjustment instructions on page 16.

When the cake is cooked, place the lemon juice, icing sugar and gin in a separate bowl or mug and microwave on full power for 30 seconds, then whisk to ensure the icing sugar has dissolved and pour over the cake.

Remove the lining paper and serve straight away for best results. This cake must be eaten on the day it is made.

To make more portions of this cake simply double or triple the above quantities and then cook each portion separately in individual mugs.

**SERVES:** 1
**PREPARATION TIME: 5 minutes**
**COOKING TIME: 3 minutes**
  **(850W microwave)**
**EQUIPMENT: 1 microwave-proof mug (400ml/15fl oz/1½ cups), whisk, baking parchment**

45g/1½oz/2 tbsp butter, plus extra for greasing
60g/2oz/3 tbsp self-raising/self-rising flour, sifted
60g/2oz/2 tbsp caster/superfine sugar
30ml/1fl oz/2 tbsp milk
20g/¾oz/1 tbsp beaten egg
Zest of 1 lemon
For the drizzle:
Juice of 1 lemon
30g/1oz/1 tbsp icing/confectioners' sugar
15ml/1 tbsp gin

## HINTS AND TIPS
To decorate you can make candied lemon peel by boiling 60g/2oz/2 tbsp granulated/white sugar in 120ml/4fl oz/½ cup water to make a thin syrup. Add thin strips of lemon zest and simmer for 5 minutes until soft.

I love cakes with powerful hints of chocolate and coffee and this little cake makes a great treat. The coffee and chocolate flavoured sponge is light and is topped with a rich coffee buttercream. Decorate with chocolate coffee beans for a true caffeine hit.

# MOCHA CHOCO WITH ESPRESSO

SERVES: **1**
PREPARATION TIME: **5 minutes**
COOKING TIME: **3 minutes**
   (850W microwave)
EQUIPMENT: **1 microwave-proof mug (400ml/ 15fl oz/1½ cups), whisk, baking parchment, piping/pastry bag fitted with a small star nozzle**

45g/1½oz/2 tbsp butter, plus extra for greasing
60g/2oz/3 tbsp self-raising/ self-rising flour, sifted
30g/1oz/1 tbsp cocoa powder, sifted
60g/2oz/2 tbsp caster/ superfine sugar
30ml/1fl oz/2 tbsp milk
20g/¾oz/1 tbsp beaten egg
5ml/1 tsp coffee extract

For the icing:
120g/4oz/1 cup icing/ confectioners' sugar, sifted
30g/1oz/1½ tbsp butter, softened
20ml/4 tsp espresso coffee
Chocolate-covered coffee beans to decorate

Place the butter in a heatproof bowl in the microwave and heat on full power for about 40 seconds until it has melted then leave it to cool.

Place the flour, cocoa, sugar, milk, egg, melted butter and coffee extract in a mixing bowl and whisk together until everything is incorporated. Make sure that there are no lumps of flour. The batter should be thick and runny.

Cut a piece of baking parchment into a rectangle about 2.5cm/1in taller than your mug and slightly wider than the circumference of your mug. Grease the mug with a little butter and place the baking parchment inside so that it lies flat around the sides of the mug with a little paper overlapping at the join. Pour the batter into the mug.

Cook on full power in a microwave (850W) for 3 minutes until the cake springs back to your touch. If you have a different power microwave, use the cooking time adjustment instructions on page 16. Leave to cool then remove the lining paper.

For the icing, place the icing sugar, butter and espresso coffee in a mixing bowl and whisk until the icing is thick and holds a stiff peak, adding a little extra coffee if the icing is too stiff. Spoon the icing into the piping bag and pipe small stars of icing over the top of the cooled cake. Decorate with the chocolate-covered coffee beans. This cake must be eaten on the day it is made.

## HINTS AND TIPS
If you do not have chocolate-covered coffee beans for the decoration, top with grated chocolate curls instead. You can easily make these by pulling a vegetable peeler along the edge of a bar of chocolate.

Salted caramel is so popular now and this is one of my favourite desserts to make for a rich and indulgent treat. You need to make the caramel sauce first because it is used to flavour the cake as well as to pour over when serving. You can serve this cake with clotted cream or crème fraîche or even a scoop of ice cream.

# SALTED CARAMEL PUDDING

**SERVES: 1**
**PREPARATION TIME: 5 minutes**
**COOKING TIME: 3 minutes**
(850W microwave)
**EQUIPMENT: 1 microwave-proof mug (400ml/15fl oz/1½ cups), whisk, baking parchment**

45g/1½oz/2 tbsp butter, plus extra for greasing
60g/3oz/3 tbsp self-raising/self-rising flour, sifted
30g/1oz/1 tbsp ground almonds

60g/2oz/2 tbsp soft light brown sugar
30ml/1fl oz/2 tbsp milk
20g/¾oz/1 tbsp beaten egg
For the sauce:
60g/2oz/2 tbsp caster/superfine sugar
45g/1½oz/2 tbsp butter
60ml/2fl oz/¼ cup double/heavy cream
2.5ml/½ tsp salt
Clotted cream, crème fraîche or single/light cream, to serve

Begin by making the sauce. Place the caster sugar, butter, cream and salt in a microwaveproof bowl and microwave on full power (850W) for 1 minute then remove from the microwave and stir well. Return to the microwave and cook for a further minute on full power. Remove from the microwave carefully as the sauce will be hot, stir well and set aside.

Place the butter in a heatproof bowl in the microwave and heat on full power for about 40 seconds until it has melted then leave it to cool.

Place the flour, ground almonds, sugar, milk, egg, melted butter and one tablespoon of the salted caramel sauce in a mixing bowl and whisk together until everything is incorporated. Make sure that there are no lumps of flour. The batter should be thick and runny.

Cut a piece of baking parchment into a rectangle about 2.5cm/1in taller than your mug and slightly wider than the circumference of your mug. Grease the mug with a little butter and place the baking parchment inside so that it lies flat around the sides of the mug with a little paper overlapping at the join. Pour the batter into the mug.

Cook on full power in a microwave (850W) for 3 minutes until the cake springs back to your touch. If you have a different power microwave, use the cooking time adjustment instructions on page 16.

Leave the cake to cool for a minute, then remove the lining paper, slide a knife around the edge of the mug and invert the mug into a bowl or on to a plate. Serve with the caramel sauce and a spoonful or two of clotted cream, crème fraîche or single cream. This sponge is best eaten on the day it is made.

To make more portions of this cake simply double or triple the above quantities and then cook each portion separately in individual mugs.

## HINTS AND TIPS
For a darker and richer caramel you can replace the light brown sugar in the sponge and the caster/superfine sugar in the sauce with dark muscovado/molasses sugar if you wish.

Vibrant green pistachio nuts are one of my favourite baking ingredients – they have a delicious perfumed flavour and add a good crunchy texture to a cake. The heat from the cake will melt the white chocolate buttons for the decoration in no time at all. If you do not have pistachios you can substitute other nuts of your choosing, such as pecans or hazelnuts.

# PISTACHIO AND WHITE CHOCOLATE CAKE

SERVES: 1
PREPARATION TIME: 5 minutes
COOKING TIME: 3 minutes
   (850W microwave)
EQUIPMENT: food processor,
   1 microwaveproof mug
   (400ml/15fl oz/1½ cups),
   whisk, baking parchment

60g/2oz/2 tbsp shelled pistachio nuts
45g/1½oz/2 tbsp butter, plus extra for greasing
60g/2oz/3 tbsp self-raising/self-rising flour, sifted
60g/2oz/2 tbsp caster/superfine sugar
30ml/1fl oz/2 tbsp milk
20g/¾oz/1 tbsp beaten egg
45g/1½oz/2 tbsp white chocolate buttons

Blitz the pistachio nuts in a food processor until they are finely chopped.

Place the butter in a heatproof bowl in the microwave and heat on full power for about 40 seconds until it has melted then leave it to cool.

Place the flour, sugar, milk, egg and melted butter in a mixing bowl and whisk together until everything is incorporated. Make sure that there are no lumps of flour. The batter should be thick and runny. Stir in most of the ground pistachio nuts, reserving a few for decoration. Stir in half of the white chocolate buttons, reserving the rest for decoration.

Cut a piece of baking parchment into a rectangle about 2.5cm/1in taller than your mug and slightly wider than the circumference of your mug. Grease the mug with a little butter and place the baking parchment inside so that it lies flat around the sides of the mug with a little paper overlapping at the join.

Pour the batter into the mug. Cook on full power in a microwave (850W) for 3 minutes until the cake springs back to your touch. If you have a different power microwave, use the cooking time adjustment instructions on page 16.

When the cake is cooked, place the reserved white chocolate buttons on top of the cake whilst still hot and leave for a few minutes to melt, then sprinkle with the reserved pistachio nuts. Remove the lining paper. The cake should be eaten on the day it is made.

## HINTS AND TIPS
If making a gluten- or dairy-free version make sure the chocolate buttons are free from gluten or dairy.

This marble cake is made with vanilla and chocolate sponge cake and looks particularly pretty when made in a glass mug so that you can see the different colours. You can use this method to make a rainbow using different food colourings, if you prefer, for equally spectacular results.

# BLACK AND WHITE CHOCOLATE CAKE

SERVES: **1**
PREPARATION TIME: **5 minutes**
COOKING TIME: **3 minutes**
  **(850W microwave)**
EQUIPMENT: **1 microwaveproof glass (400ml/15fl oz/ 1½ cups), whisk, baking parchment, piping/pastry bag fitted with large star nozzle**

45g/1½oz/2 tbsp butter, plus extra for greasing
60g/2oz/3 tbsp self-raising/ self-rising flour, sifted
60g/2oz/2 tbsp caster/ superfine sugar
30ml/1fl oz/2 tbsp milk
20g/¾oz/1 tbsp beaten egg
5ml/1 tsp vanilla extract
20g/⅔oz/1 tbsp cocoa powder, sifted

For the frosting:
115g/4oz/1 cup icing/ confectioners' sugar, sifted
10g/1oz/1 tbsp cocoa powder, sifted
20g/2oz/2½ tbsp butter, softened
White chocolate hearts or other white chocolate decorations (optional)

Place the butter in a heatproof bowl in the microwave and heat on full power for about 40 seconds until it has melted then leave it to cool.

Place the flour, sugar, milk, egg and melted butter in a mixing bowl and whisk together until everything is incorporated. Divide the mixture into two bowls and stir the vanilla into one half of the mixture and the cocoa powder into the other. Whisk in so that the cocoa and vanilla are incorporated.

Grease and line the glass following the instructions on page 19. Pour the batter into the glass a spoonful at a time, alternating the vanilla and chocolate batters so that you have marbled layers of different coloured batter.

Cook on full power in a microwave (850W) for 3 minutes until the cake springs back to your touch. If you have a different power microwave, use the cooking time adjustment instructions on page 16.

Place the frosting ingredients together in a bowl and whisk until smooth, adding a little milk if the mixture is too stiff, making sure there are no lumps. Spoon the frosting into piping bag fitted with a large star nozzle. When the cake is cool and you have removed the lining paper, pipe a large swirl of the frosting over the top. Decorate with the white chocolate hearts or other decorations, if using. The cake should be eaten on the day it is made.

To make more portions of this cake simply double or triple the above quantities and then cook each portion separately in individual mugs.

This little cake is a hug in a mug – it is rich and indulgent with a delicious Irish cream sauce and topped with a spoonful of cream. The alcohol in the sponge means it needs a slightly shorter cooking time compared to a regular mug cake.

# IRISH CREAM LIQUEUR CAKE

SERVES: **1**
PREPARATION TIME: **5 minutes**
COOKING TIME: **2½ minutes**
    **(850W microwave)**
EQUIPMENT: **1 microwave-
    proof mug (400ml/
    15fl oz/1½ cups), whisk**

45g/1½oz/2 tbsp butter
60g/2oz/3 tbsp self-raising/
    self-rising flour, sifted
60g/2oz/2 tbsp caster/
    superfine sugar

15ml/½fl oz/1 tbsp milk
15ml/½fl oz/1 tbsp Irish cream
    liqueur, such as Baileys
20g/¾ oz/1 tbsp beaten egg
For the pouring sauce:
30g/1oz/1 tbsp caster/
    superfine sugar
30g/1oz/1½ tbsp butter
60ml/4 tbsp Irish cream liqueur,
    such as Baileys
15ml/1 tbsp clotted cream or
    extra thick double/heavy
    cream, to serve

Place the butter in a heatproof bowl in the microwave and heat on full power for about 40 seconds until it has melted then leave it to cool.

Place the flour, sugar, milk, Irish cream liqueur, egg and melted butter in a mixing bowl and whisk together until everything is incorporated. Make sure that there are no lumps of flour. The batter should be thick and runny.

Pour the batter into the mug until it is no more than two-thirds full. Do not overfill the mug otherwise it may overflow when cooking.

Cook on full power in a microwave (850W) for 2½ minutes until the cake springs back to your touch. If you have a different power microwave, use the cooking time adjustment instructions on page 16.

When the cake is cooked, prepare the sauce: place the caster sugar, butter and liqueur in a microwaveproof bowl and microwave on full power (850W) for one minute, then remove from the microwave and whisk well. Allow the sauce to cool for a short while and then pour over the cake and top with the cream. Serve straight away.

To make more portions of this cake simply double or triple the above quantities and then cook each portion separately in individual mugs.

### HINTS AND TIPS
If making a gluten-free version of this cake using the recipe on page 14, make sure that the brand of Irish cream liqueur you use is gluten-free. For dairy-free cakes, store-bought Irish cream liqueurs contain dairy although other non-cream liqueurs (like some coffee liqueurs) can work well too, giving a different flavour.

In January each year I love to celebrate Burns Night with all things traditionally Scottish and certainly plenty of whisky! This little cake is a delicious taste of Scotland made with tangy marmalade and glazed with a whisky syrup. It makes a perfect dessert served with custard, see page 45 for a recipe.

# WHISKY AND MARMALADE SYRUP CAKE

Place the butter in a heatproof bowl in the microwave and heat on full power for about 40 seconds until it has melted then leave it to cool.

Place the flour, soft light brown sugar, milk, egg, melted butter, marmalade and orange zest in a mixing bowl and whisk together until everything is incorporated. Make sure that there are no lumps of flour. The batter should be thick and runny.

Cut a piece of baking parchment into a rectangle about 2.5cm/1in taller than your mug and slightly wider than the circumference of your mug. Grease the mug with a little butter and place the baking parchment inside so that it lies flat around the sides of the mug with a little paper overlapping at the join. Pour the batter into the mug.

Cook on full power in a microwave (850W) for 3 minutes until the cake springs back to your touch. If you have a different power microwave, use the cooking time adjustment instructions on page 16.

When the cake is cooked, remove from the microwave, then place the soft light brown sugar, whisky and marmalade in a separate bowl or mug and microwave (850W) on full power for 1 minute, then whisk to blend everything together. Pour a small amount of the syrup over the cake and brush with a pastry brush to glaze the top of the cake. When you are ready to eat, press a spoon into the centre of the cake and pour in the remaining sauce to give the cake a gooey centre. Remove the lining paper and serve straight away warm for best results. The cake should be eaten on the day it is made.

SERVES: **1**
PREPARATION TIME: **5 minutes**
COOKING TIME: **3 minutes**
  **(850W microwave)**
EQUIPMENT: **1 microwaveproof mug (400ml/15fl oz/1½ cups), whisk, baking parchment, pastry brush**

45g/1½oz/2 tbsp butter, plus extra for greasing
60g/2oz/3 tbsp self-raising/self-rising flour, sifted
60g/2oz/2 tbsp soft light brown sugar
30ml/1fl oz/2 tbsp milk
20g/¾oz/1 tbsp beaten egg
30g/1oz/1 tbsp fine shred marmalade
2.5ml/½ tsp orange zest
For the whisky orange sauce:
30g/1oz/1 tbsp soft light brown sugar
15ml/½fl oz/1 tbsp whisky
30g/1oz/1 tbsp fine shred marmalade

# JUST FOR KIDS

Microwave baking is ideal for children as there is no hot oven to contend with and the recipes are so easy to prepare that children can easily make them too. This chapter contains many fun cakes, such as cola bottle and marshmallow cakes, or for kids who love chocolate why not try the chocolate hazelnut cake topped with large swirls of frosting.

I learnt a lot of things whilst writing this book, one of which is that large marshmallows have a tendency to explode in microwaves! Well not explode exactly, but expand a lot which can result in a gooey mess like none that I have experienced before. It is therefore important only to use mini marshmallows in this recipe. If you want you can bake in glasses – I love to see the pink sponge with the marshmallows melted on top – almost like a milkshake.

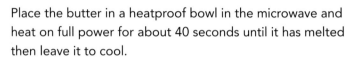

# MARSHMALLOW CAKE

SERVES: **1**
PREPARATION TIME: **5 minutes**
COOKING TIME: **3 minutes**
    (**850W microwave**)
EQUIPMENT: **1 microwave-proof mug (400ml/ 15fl oz/1½ cups), whisk, baking parchment**

45g/1½oz/2 tbsp butter, plus extra for greasing
60g/2oz/3 tbsp self-raising/ self-rising flour, sifted
60g/2oz/2 tbsp caster/ superfine sugar
30ml/1fl oz/2 tbsp milk
20g/¾oz/1 tbsp beaten egg
5ml/1 tsp vanilla extract
A few drops of pink or red food colouring
30g/1oz/2 tbsp mini marshmallows

Place the butter in a heatproof bowl in the microwave and heat on full power for about 40 seconds until it has melted then leave it to cool.

Place the flour, sugar, milk, egg, melted butter, vanilla and a few drops of food colouring in a mixing bowl and whisk together until everything is incorporated. Make sure that there are no lumps of flour. The batter should be thick and runny. Stir in half of the marshmallows reserving the remainder for the topping.

Cut a piece of baking parchment into a rectangle about 2.5cm/1in taller than your mug and slightly wider than the circumference of your mug. Grease the mug with a little butter and place the baking parchment inside so that it lies flat around the sides of the mug with a little paper overlapping at the join. Pour the batter into the mug.

Cook on full power in a microwave (850W) for 2 minutes 30 seconds until the cake springs back to your touch. If you have a different power microwave, use the cooking time adjustment instructions on page 16.

Remove the cake from the microwave and place the reserved marshmallows on top then return to the microwave and cook for a further 20 seconds until the marshmallows just begin to melt. Remove the lining paper and serve the cake straight away whilst still warm.

### HINTS AND TIPS
If making a gluten- or dairy-free version, make sure that the marshmallows are gluten- or dairy-free. Check the labelling carefully.

These clever little cakes are baked in paper cups. You could also hunt out ice cream cornet cups for an all-edible cake – if so it is important to use flat bottom cornets so that they stand and bake evenly whilst cooking. This recipe makes four cakes, as only a small amount of batter is needed in each cup, so they are perfect for last-minute children's parties.

# ICE CREAM CAKES

Place the butter in a heatproof bowl in the microwave and heat on full power for about 40 seconds until it has melted then leave it to cool.

Place the flour, sugar, milk, egg, melted butter and vanilla in a mixing bowl and whisk together until everything is incorporated. Make sure that there are no lumps of flour. The batter should be thick and runny.

Cut a piece of baking parchment into four rectangles about 2.5cm/1in taller than your cups and slightly wider than the circumference of your cups. Grease the cups with a little butter and place the baking parchment rectangles inside so that they lie flat around the sides of the cups with a little paper overlapping at the join. Divide the batter between the four paper cups making sure that they are no more than half full.

Cook two cups at a time on full power in a microwave (850W) for 1 minute until the cakes spring back to your touch. If you have a different power microwave, use the cooking time adjustment instructions on page 16. Repeat with the two remaining cups. Leave the cakes to cool before removing the lining paper.

When the cakes are cooled, make the icing by placing the icing sugar, butter and milk in a mixing bowl and whisking to stiff peaks for a few minutes until the icing is very thick and creamy. Add the milk gradually as you may not need it all, or if the icing is too stiff add a little extra milk. Spoon the icing into the piping bag and pipe a large swirl of icing on top of each cake. Cut the flakes in half and press half a flake into each cake to make them look like ice creams. Finally top the cakes with some sugar sprinkles. These cakes must be eaten on the day they are made.

MAKES: 4
PREPARATION TIME: 10 minutes
COOKING TIME: 2 minutes
   (850W microwave)
EQUIPMENT: whisk, 4 paper cups, baking parchment, piping/pastry bag fitted with a large star nozzle

45g/1½oz/2 tbsp butter, plus extra for greasing
60g/2oz/3 tbsp self-raising/ self-rising flour, sifted
60g/2oz/2 tbsp caster/ superfine sugar
30ml/1fl oz/2 tbsp milk
20g/¾oz/1 tbsp beaten egg
5ml/1 tsp vanilla extract
For the icing:
220g/8oz/2 scant cups icing/ confectioners' sugar, sifted
60g/2oz/3 tbsp butter, softened
15ml/1 tbsp milk
2 chocolate flakes and sugar sprinkles, to decorate

Fizzy cola bottles were a childhood favourite of mine and although it is probably a bad thing to admit they occasionally still end up in my shopping basket today! Kids will love these cakes that they can prepare themselves with a little adult supervision.

# COLA BOTTLE CAKE

Place the butter in a heatproof bowl in the microwave and heat on full power for about 40 seconds until it has melted then leave it to cool.

In a bowl, whisk together the melted butter, flour, sugar, cola, cocoa powder and egg until everything is incorporated. Make sure that there are no lumps of flour. The batter should be thick and runny.

Pour the batter into the mug until it is no more than three-quarters full. Do not overfill the mug otherwise it will overflow when cooking.

Cook on full power in a microwave (850W) for 3 minutes until the cake springs back to your touch. If you have a different power microwave, use the cooking time adjustment instructions on page 16.

For the icing, whisk together the butter, cream cheese, cola and icing sugar until you have a smooth, thick icing (add the cola gradually as you may not need it all). Spoon the icing into the piping bag fitted with a large star nozzle. Pipe a large swirl of icing over the cake and top with the jelly cola bottles. This cake is best eaten on the day it is made.

To make more portions of this cake simply double or triple the above quantities and then cook each portion separately in individual mugs.

SERVES: 1
PREPARATION TIME: 5 minutes
COOKING TIME: 3 minutes
 (850W microwave)
EQUIPMENT: 1 microwave-
 proof mug (400ml/
 15fl oz/1½ cups), whisk,
 piping/pastry bag fitted
 with a large star nozzle

45g/1½oz/2 tbsp butter
60g/2oz/3 tbsp self-raising/
 self-rising flour, sifted
60g/2oz/2 tbsp caster/
 superfine sugar
30ml/1fl oz/2 tbsp cola
20g/⅔oz/1 tbsp cocoa
 powder, sifted
20g/¾oz/1 tbsp beaten egg
For the icing:
25g/1oz/2 tbsp unsalted butter
25g/1oz/2 tbsp cream cheese
10ml/2 tsp cola
100g/3¾oz/scant 1 cup icing/
 confectioners' sugar
Jelly cola bottles (fizzy or plain),
 to decorate

## HINTS AND TIPS

Check the ingredients on the cola bottles to ensure that they do not contain any allergens if you are making dairy- or gluten-free versions of this cake. If you put the cola bottles on to the cake whilst they are still warm, the cola bottles will become warm, gooey and utterly delicious!

One of my favourite things to eat are Reese's peanut butter cups – naughty but so very nice with wicked peanut butter filling coated in milk chocolate. So what better cake for me to make in the microwave than this delicious peanut butter sponge, topped with mini peanut butter cups that melt on the warm cake to give a gooey topping. Topped with a generous scoop of ice cream whilst the cake is still warm gives a perfect hot and cold dessert.

# PEANUT BUTTER MUG CAKE

Place the butter in a heatproof bowl in the microwave and heat on full power for about 40 seconds until it has melted then leave to cool.

Place the flour, sugar, milk, egg, melted butter and peanut butter in a mixing bowl and whisk together until everything is incorporated. Make sure that there are no lumps of flour. The batter should be thick and runny.

Chop the peanut butter cups into small pieces and stir two-thirds into the batter. Pour the batter into the mug until it is no more than three-quarters full. Do not overfill the mug otherwise it will overflow when cooking.

Cook on full power in a microwave (850W) for 3 minutes until the cake springs back to your touch. If you have a different power microwave, use the cooking time adjustment instructions on page 16.

Whilst the cake is still warm, sprinkle the reserved chopped peanut butter cups over the top. Serve with a scoop of ice cream and sprinkled with roughly chopped salted peanuts if you like. This cake is best eaten on the day it is made.

To make more portions of this cake simply double or triple the above quantities and then cook each portion separately in individual mugs.

**SERVES: 1**
**PREPARATION TIME: 5 minutes**
**COOKING TIME: 3 minutes**
  **(850W microwave)**
**EQUIPMENT: 1 microwaveproof**
  **mug (400ml/15fl oz/**
  **1½ cups), whisk**

45g/1½oz/2 tbsp butter
60g/2oz/3 tbsp self-raising/
  self-rising flour, sifted
60g/2oz/2 tbsp caster/
  superfine sugar

30ml/1fl oz/2 tbsp milk
20g/¾oz/1 tbsp beaten egg
30ml/2 tbsp peanut butter
5 mini Reese's peanut
  butter cups
A scoop of ice cream and
  15g/½oz salted peanuts,
  roughly chopped,
  to serve (optional)

## HINTS AND TIPS

If making a gluten or dairy-free version, in place of the peanut butter cups use gluten-free chocolate or dairy-free chocolate, chopped into small pieces. Add a few salted peanuts to the batter for added crunch, if you wish.

My friend Maren loves Nutella and I made this cake just for her. If you love Nutella then I have no doubt you will enjoy it too. It is packed with crunchy hazelnuts and has a gooey Nutella centre. Topped with a yummy hazelnut frosting and a hazelnut chocolate, this cake is nutalicious!

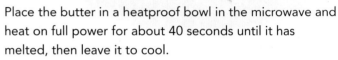

# CHOCOLATE HAZELNUT CAKE

**SERVES:** 1
**PREPARATION TIME:** 5 minutes
**COOKING TIME:** 3 minutes
  (850W microwave)
**EQUIPMENT:** 1 microwave-
  proof mug (400ml/
  15fl oz/1½ cups), whisk,
  baking parchment,
  piping/pastry bag fitted
  with a large star nozzle

45g/1½oz/2 tbsp butter, plus
  extra for greasing
60g/2oz/3 tbsp self-raising/
  self-rising flour, sifted
20g/⅔oz/1 tbsp cocoa
  powder, sifted
60g/2oz/2 tbsp caster/
  superfine sugar
30ml/1fl oz/2 tbsp milk
20g/¾oz/1 tbsp beaten egg

60g/2oz/2 tbsp chocolate
  hazelnut spread,
  such as Nutella
20g/¾oz/1 tbsp chopped
  toasted hazelnuts
For the frosting:
20g/⅔oz/1 tbsp butter,
  softened
60g/2oz/4 tbsp icing/
  confectioners' sugar, sifted
30g/1oz/1tbsp chocolate
  hazelnut spread,
  such as Nutella
1 Ferrero Rocher chocolate
Toasted chopped hazelnuts,
  to sprinkle

Place the butter in a heatproof bowl in the microwave and heat on full power for about 40 seconds until it has melted, then leave it to cool.

Place the flour, cocoa, sugar, milk, egg, melted butter and 15ml/1 tbsp of the chocolate hazelnut spread in a mixing bowl and whisk together until everything is incorporated. Fold in the chopped toasted hazelnuts. Make sure that there are no lumps of flour. The batter should be thick and runny.

Cut a piece of baking parchment into a rectangle about 2.5cm/1in taller than your mug and slightly wider than the circumference of your mug. Grease the mug with a little butter and place the baking parchment inside so that it lies flat around the sides of the mug with a little paper overlapping at the join.

Pour the batter into the mug. Place the remaining spoonful of chocolate hazelnut spread into the centre of the batter. It will sink when it cooks, giving a gooey centre.

Cook on full power in a microwave (850W) for 3 minutes until the cake springs back to your touch. If you have a different power microwave, use the cooking time adjustment instructions on page 16.

Leave the cake to cool and then remove the lining paper. For the icing, whisk together the butter, icing sugar and chocolate hazelnut spread until you have a thick and creamy icing. Spoon into the piping bag and pipe a large swirl of icing on top of the cooled cake. Decorate the top of the cake with toasted hazelnuts and the Ferrero Rocher. The cake should be eaten on the day it is made.

To make more portions of this cake simply double or triple the above quantities and then cook each portion separately in individual mugs.

One of the things I love to do most is to decorate cakes – piled high with swirls of icing and pretty sugar decorations. Even when you are making a quick mug cake you can still have fun icing and decorating. This little orange-flavoured cake looks so pretty topped with pale green icing and sugar butterflies and flowers it makes a perfect summer's day cake or a last-minute birthday cake!

# PRETTY BUTTERFLY CAKE

Place the butter in a heatproof bowl in the microwave and heat on full power for about 40 seconds until it has melted then leave it to cool.

Place the flour, sugar, milk, egg, melted butter and orange zest in a mixing bowl and whisk together until everything is incorporated. Make sure that there are no lumps of flour. The batter should be thick and runny.

Cut a piece of baking parchment into a rectangle about 2.5cm/1in taller than your mug and slightly wider than the circumference of your mug. Grease the mug with a little butter and place the baking parchment inside so that it lies flat around the sides of the mug with a little paper overlapping at the join. Pour the batter into the mug.

Cook on full power in a microwave (850W) for 3 minutes until the cake springs back to your touch. If you have a different power microwave, use the cooking time adjustment instructions on page 16.

When the cake is cooked, place almost all of the orange juice (reserving a few teaspoons for the icing) and icing sugar in a separate bowl or mug and microwave on full power for 30 seconds, then whisk to ensure the icing sugar has dissolved and pour over the cake as a drizzle.

Allow the cake to cool and remove the lining paper. For the icing mix the icing sugar with a few teaspoons of orange juice until you have thick icing, using a little extra water if the icing is too thick. Colour very pale green using a small amount of food colouring. Spread over the top of the cake using a round-bladed knife, then decorate with the sugar flowers and butterflies. The cake should be eaten on the day it is made.

To make more portions of this cake simply double or triple the above quantities and then cook each portion separately in individual mugs.

**SERVES: 1**
**PREPARATION TIME: 5 minutes**
**COOKING TIME: 3½ minutes (850W microwave)**
**EQUIPMENT: 1 microwave-proof mug (400ml/ 15fl oz/1½ cups), whisk, baking parchment**

45g/1½oz/2 tbsp butter, plus extra for greasing
60g/2oz/3 tbsp self-raising/ self-rising flour, sifted
60g/2oz/2 tbsp caster/ superfine sugar
30ml/1fl oz/2 tbsp milk
20g/¾oz/1 tbsp beaten egg
Zest and juice of 1 small orange
30g/1oz/1 tbsp icing/ confectioners' sugar
For the icing:
60g/2oz/2 tbsp icing/ confectioners' sugar, sifted
5–10ml/1–2 tsp orange juice (from the orange above)
A drop of green food colouring
Sugar butterflies and sugar flowers, to decorate

# FESTIVE MUG CAKES

Mug cakes are not just for everyday but can also be used as perfect miniature celebration cakes on festive occasions. This chapter covers all your seasonal cake requirements – from Halloween and Thanksgiving cakes to Christmas chocolate logs. There is even a mini birthday cake for last-minute birthday parties.

Treacle toffee was my Granddad Goodwin's favourite – he used to be given boxes and boxes of Thornton's Treacle Toffee for Christmas that would last him the whole year! This recipe is a deliciously rich toffee sponge topped with the treacle toffee sauce. I love to serve it on bonfire night for everyone to eat warm in mugs outdoors as they watch the fireworks.

# BONFIRE TREACLE CAKE

Place the butter in a heatproof bowl in the microwave and heat on full power for about 40 seconds until it has melted then leave it to cool.

Next make the sauce. Unwrap the toffees from their wrappers and place in a bowl with the butter and milk. Microwave on full power for about 2 minutes, stirring halfway through. Take care as the liquid will be hot. Whisk the mixture until you have a smooth toffee sauce. Leave to one side whilst you make the cake.

Place the flour, sugar, milk, egg, melted butter, treacle and ground cinnamon in a mixing bowl and whisk together until everything is incorporated. Make sure that there are no lumps of flour. The batter should be thick and runny.

Cut a piece of baking parchment into a rectangle about 2.5cm/1in taller than your mug and slightly wider than the circumference of your mug. Grease the mug with a little butter and place the baking parchment inside so that it lies flat around the sides of the mug with a little paper overlapping at the join. Pour the batter into the mug.

Cook on full power in a microwave (850W) for 3 minutes until the cake springs back to your touch. If you have a different power microwave, use the cooking time adjustment instructions on page 16.

When the cake is cooked, remove the lining paper pour the toffee sauce over and serve, allowing the cake to cool for a few minutes before serving. The cake should be eaten on the day it is made and is best eaten warm.

### HINTS AND TIPS

If you aren't able to find treacle toffees you can substitute regular toffees for equally delicious results.

SERVES: **1**
PREPARATION TIME: **5 minutes**
COOKING TIME: **5 minutes** (850W microwave)
EQUIPMENT: **1 microwave-proof mug (400ml/ 15fl oz/1½ cups), whisk, baking parchment**

45g/1½oz/2 tbsp butter, plus extra for greasing
60g/2oz/3 tbsp self-raising/ self-rising flour, sifted
60g/2oz/2 tbsp soft dark brown sugar
30ml/1fl oz/2 tbsp milk
20g/¾oz/1 tbsp beaten egg
15ml/½fl oz/1 tbsp treacle/ molasses
2.5ml/½ tsp ground cinnamon
For the sauce:
4 treacle toffees
20g/¾oz/1 tbsp butter
15ml/½fl oz/1 tbsp milk

At Halloween and Thanksgiving I love to make cakes flavoured with seasonal pumpkin and traditional spices. These little cakes are perfect as they are quick to prepare and decorate and can then be served as a centrepiece for a party.

# PUMPKIN PIE CAKE

**SERVES: 1**
**PREPARATION TIME: 5 minutes**
**COOKING TIME: 3 minutes**
   (850W microwave)
**EQUIPMENT: 1 microwave-**
   **proof mug (400ml/**
   **15fl oz/1½ cups), whisk**

45g/1½oz/2 tbsp butter, plus
   extra for greasing
60g/2oz/3 tbsp self-raising/
   self-rising flour, sifted
60g/2oz/2 tbsp caster/
   superfine sugar
20g/¾oz/1 tbsp beaten egg
30ml/1fl oz/2 tbsp milk
2.5ml/½ tsp ground cinnamon
2.5ml/½ tsp ground ginger
2.5ml/½ tsp vanilla extract
15ml/1 tbsp pumpkin purée
30g/1oz/1 tbsp white
   chocolate chunks or chips
For the icing:
45g/1½oz/2 tbsp icing/
   confectioners' sugar, sifted
5ml/1 tsp orange juice
A few drops of orange food
   colouring
1 small chocolate stick, such as
   mini orange-flavoured
   Matchmakers
1 green fondant leaf
   decoration

Place the butter in a heatproof bowl in the microwave and heat on full power for about 40 seconds until it has melted then leave it to cool.

Mix together the flour, sugar, egg, milk, cinnamon, ginger, vanilla and pumpkin purée and whisk until everything is incorporated. Make sure that there are no lumps of flour. The batter should be thick and runny. Fold in the white chocolate chunks or chips.

Grease and line the mug following the instructions on page 19. Pour the batter in until it is no more than three-quarters full.

Cook the mug on full power in a microwave (850W) for 3 minutes until the cakes spring back to your touch. If you have a different power microwave, use the cooking time adjustment instructions on page 16.

Remove the lining paper, then mix the icing sugar with the orange juice and orange food colouring until you have a smooth icing, adding a little extra water if necessary, and spread over the top of the cake.

Press a small piece of chocolate stick into the centre of the cake and place a green fondant leaf decoration next to the stick. Leave the icing to set before serving. This cake is best eaten on the day it is made.

## HINTS AND TIPS
If you want to turn the cake out you can make it in round-bottomed teacups (make sure that they are microwaveproof before using) and then invert on to a serving plate so that you have a pumpkin shape. Ice and decorate the cake in the same way as above. The recipe will make enough for 2 teacups as they are smaller than mugs.

For a last-minute Halloween celebration these little orange-flavoured chocolate chip cakes make a perfect indulgent treat. The swirled orange and black icing is a striking decoration and for added drama why not try some toy spiders!

# HALLOWEEN CAKE

Place the butter in a heatproof bowl in the microwave and heat on full power for about 40 seconds until it has melted then leave it to cool.

Place the flour, sugar, milk, egg, melted butter, orange extract and orange food colouring in a mixing bowl and whisk together until everything is incorporated. Fold in the chocolate chips. Make sure that there are no lumps of flour. The batter should be thick and runny. Grease and line the mug, see page 19. Pour the batter into the mug.

Cook on full power in a microwave (850W) for 3 minutes until the cake springs back to your touch. If you have a different power microwave, use the cooking time adjustment instructions on page 16. Leave the cake to cool completely and remove the lining paper.

For the icing, whisk together the icing sugar, milk and softened butter until you have a thick icing, adding the milk gradually as you may not need it all. If the icing is too stiff add a little extra milk. Divide the icing into two separate bowls. Add orange food colouring to one and black to the other. Spoon the orange and black icing into the piping bag, one down each side of the bag as shown. Pipe a swirl of icing on to the top of the cake. This cake must be eaten on the day it is made. Remove any toy spiders before eating!

## HINTS AND TIPS

This recipe can be adapted for any number of different flavours and colours. One alternative is substituting peppermint extract for the orange, and using green food colouring in the cake mixture and half the icing, for a ghoulish green and black tasty treat.

SERVES: 1
PREPARATION TIME: **5 minutes**
COOKING TIME: **3 minutes
(850W microwave)**
EQUIPMENT: **1 microwave-proof mug (400ml/15fl oz/1½ cups), whisk, piping/pastry bag fitted with a large star nozzle**

45g/1½oz/2 tbsp butter, plus extra for greasing
60g/2oz/3 tbsp self-raising/self-rising flour, sifted
60g/2oz/2 tbsp caster/superfine sugar
30ml/1fl oz/2 tbsp milk
20g/¾oz/1 tbsp beaten egg
2.5ml/½ tsp finely grated orange zest
A few drops of orange food colouring
30g/1oz/1 tbsp chocolate chips

For the icing:
120g/4oz/1 cup icing/confectioners' sugar, sifted, plus extra for dusting
15ml/1 tbsp milk
60g/2oz/2 tbsp butter, softened
A few drops of orange and black food colourings

Every year we spend a happy afternoon making our Christmas puddings to my great grandma's recipe, all taking turns to stir three times and make a wish. Often after indulging in Christmas dinner there is little room for Christmas pudding so there are always leftovers. Christmas pudding will keep for up to a year in the refrigerator so this is the perfect cake to use up your pudding. This little cake is topped with a delicious brandy butter frosting and a kitsch festive decoration.

# CHRISTMAS PUDDING CAKE

SERVES: 1
PREPARATION TIME: **5 minutes**
COOKING TIME: **3 minutes**
   **(850W microwave)**
EQUIPMENT: **1 microwave-**
   **proof mug (400ml/**
   **15fl oz/1½ cups), whisk,**
   **baking parchment**

45g/1½oz/2 tbsp butter, plus
   extra for greasing
60g/2oz/3 tbsp self-raising/
   self-rising flour, sifted

60g/2oz/2 tbsp caster/
   superfine sugar
30ml/1fl oz/2 tbsp milk
20g/¾oz/1 tbsp beaten egg
60g/2oz/2 tbsp Christmas
   pudding
1.5ml/¼ tsp ground ginger
2.5ml/½ tsp ground cinnamon
For the icing:
45g/1¾oz/2 tbsp icing/
   confectioners' sugar, sifted
   plus extra for dusting
15g/½oz/½ tbsp butter,
   softened
5–10ml/1–2 tsp brandy

Place the butter in a heatproof bowl in the microwave and heat on full power for about 40 seconds until it has melted then leave it to cool.

In a bowl, whisk together the melted butter, flour, sugar, milk and egg and whisk together until everything is incorporated. Make sure that there are no lumps of flour. The batter should be thick and runny.

Cut the Christmas pudding into small pieces and stir through the batter with the ground ginger and cinnamon.

Grease and line the mug following the instructions on page 19. Pour the batter into the mug until it is no more than three-quarters full. Do not overfill the mug otherwise it will overflow when cooking.

Cook on full power in a microwave (850W) for 3 minutes until the cake springs back to your touch. If you have a different power microwave, use the cooking time adjustment instructions on page 16. Leave to cool and remove the lining paper.

For the icing, place the icing sugar, butter and brandy in a bowl and whisk together until you have a thick and creamy icing that holds a peak when you lift the whisk. When the cake is cool, spoon the icing on top and using a fork make decorative snow patterns. Dust the cake with icing sugar for a snow effect and decorate with a Christmas decoration, if you wish. This cake is best eaten on the day it is made.

## HINTS AND TIPS
If you do not have Christmas pudding, soak 30ml/ 2 tbsp of sultanas/golden raisins in a little brandy and use instead.

At Christmas time a chocolate log is one of our favourite family traditions. This little chocolate log cake is perfect for last-minute Christmas guests as it takes no time at all to prepare. Make bark patterns using the prongs of a fork and decorate with festive decorations and a good dusting of icing sugar snow for an instant white Christmas.

# CHOCOLATE LOG

Place the butter in a heatproof bowl in the microwave and heat on full power for about 40 seconds until it has melted then leave it to cool.

Place the flour, cocoa, sugar, milk, egg and melted butter in a mixing bowl and whisk together until everything is incorporated. Make sure that there are no lumps of flour. The batter should be thick and runny.

Cut a piece of baking parchment into a rectangle about 2.5cm/1in taller than your mug and slightly wider than the circumference of your mug. Grease the mug with a little butter and place the baking parchment inside so that it lies flat around the sides of the mug with a little paper overlapping at the join.

Pour the batter into the mug and cook on full power in a microwave (850W) for 3 minutes until the cake springs back to your touch. If you have a different power microwave, use the cooking time adjustment instructions on page 16.

Leave to cool completely, then remove the cake from the mug by taking out the lining paper and sliding a knife around the cake to loosen it.

For the icing, whisk together the icing sugar, cocoa, butter and milk until the icing is smooth and thick adding the milk gradually in case you do not need it all. Cut one end of the cake off and stick it on the side of the large piece of cake using a little of the icing to make it look like a branch. Place on your serving plate or on a cake board. Using a round-bladed knife spread the icing all over the cake. Use a fork to make bark patterns over the top of the cake. Dust with icing sugar and decorate with a festive decoration. This cake must be eaten on the day it is made.

**SERVES: 2**
**PREPARATION TIME: 5 minutes**
**COOKING TIME: 3 minutes**
  **(850W microwave)**
**EQUIPMENT: 1 microwave-**
  **proof mug (400ml/**
  **15fl oz/1½ cups), whisk,**
  **baking parchment,**
  **Christmas cake**
  **decoration**

45g/1½oz/2 tbsp butter, plus
  extra for greasing
60g/2oz/3 tbsp self-raising/
  self-rising flour, sifted

30g/1oz/1 tbsp cocoa
  powder, sifted
60g/2oz/2 tbsp caster/
  superfine sugar
30ml/1fl oz/2 tbsp milk
20g/¾oz/1 tbsp beaten egg
For the icing:
120g/4oz/1 cup icing/
  confectioners' sugar, sifted,
  plus extra for dusting
30g/1oz/1 tbsp cocoa, sifted
60g/2oz/2½ tbsp butter,
  softened
15ml/1 tbsp milk

## HINTS AND TIPS
For dairy-free icing replace the butter with dairy-free spread and use almond or soya milk.

If you want to make a friend a small birthday cake and are short of time then this mug version is perfect for celebrating their special day. You could make it in a personalized mug to give to them as a present. Decorate the cake with plenty of edible gold dust and top with a party candle for a really elegant treat.

# HAPPY BIRTHDAY CAKE

Place the butter in a heatproof bowl in the microwave and heat on full power for about 40 seconds until it has melted then leave it to cool.

Place the flour, sugar, milk, egg, melted butter and vanilla in a mixing bowl and whisk together until everything is incorporated. Make sure that there are no lumps of flour. Fold in the chocolate chunks. The batter should be thick and runny.

Cut a piece of baking parchment into a rectangle about 2.5cm/1in taller than your mug and slightly wider than the circumference of your mug. Grease the mug with a little butter and place the baking parchment inside so that it lies flat around the sides of the mug with a little paper overlapping at the join.

Pour the batter into the mug. Cook on full power in a microwave (850W) for 3 minutes until the cake springs back to your touch. If you have a different power microwave, use the cooking time adjustment instructions on page 16.

Leave the cake to cool and remove the lining paper. For the icing, whisk together the butter, icing sugar, cream cheese and vanilla until you have a thick and creamy icing. Spoon into the piping bag and pipe a large swirl of icing on top of the cooled cake. Decorate with the edible gold dust or glitter and place the candle in the centre of the icing. The cake should be eaten on the day it is made.

SERVES: 1
PREPARATION TIME: 5 minutes
COOKING TIME: 3 minutes
   (850W microwave)
EQUIPMENT: 1 microwaveproof
   mug (400ml/15fl oz/
   1½ cups), whisk, baking
   parchment, piping/pastry
   bag fitted with a large
   star nozzle

45g/1½oz/2 tbsp butter, plus
   extra for greasing
60g/2oz/3 tbsp self-raising/
   self-rising flour, sifted
60g/2oz/2 tbsp caster/
   superfine sugar
30ml/1fl oz/2 tbsp milk
20g/¾oz/1 tbsp beaten egg

5ml/1 tsp vanilla extract
30g/1oz/1 tbsp milk
   chocolate chunks
For the frosting:
10ml/2 tsp butter, softened
60g/2oz/4 tbsp icing/
   confectioners' sugar, sifted
30g/1oz/1 tbsp cream cheese
2.5ml/½ tsp vanilla extract
Edible gold dust or glitter
A birthday candle and holder

**HINTS AND TIPS**
If making a dairy-free cake, decorate with a glacé icing made with 60g/2oz/2 tbsp of sifted icing/confectioners' sugar mixed with 5–10ml/1–2 tsp orange juice or water, adding a few drops of food colouring if you wish, spread over the top of the cake with a round-bladed knife. Decorate the cake with sugar sprinkles.

# NUTRITIONAL NOTES

The nutritional analysis given for each recipe is calculated for 1 mug cake. The analysis does not include optional ingredients.

**PAGE 12 Basic Plain Mug Cake** Energy 813kcal/3413kJ; Protein 9.4g; Carbohydrate 109.7g, of which sugars 65.2g; Fat 40.5g, of which saturates 24.5g; Cholesterol 175mg; Calcium 283mg; Fibre 2.5g; Sodium 533mg.

**PAGE 14 Basic Gluten-free Mug Cake** Energy 813kcal/3413kJ; Protein 9.1g; Carbohydrate 110g, of which sugars 65.5g; Fat 40.5g, of which saturates 24.5g; Cholesterol 175mg; Calcium 272mg; Fibre 2.5g; Sodium 533mg.

**PAGE 15 Basic Lactose-/Dairy-free Cake** Energy 667kcal/2812kJ; Protein 8.3g; Carbohydrate 108.7g, of which sugars 64.1g; Fat 25.2g, of which saturates 3.3g; Cholesterol 77mg; Calcium 239mg; Fibre 2.5g; Sodium 267mg.

**PAGE 26 Pearl Sugar Vanilla Cake** Energy 924kcal/3884kJ; Protein 9.6g; Carbohydrate 139g, of which sugars 94.4g; Fat 40.5g, of which saturates 24.5g; Cholesterol 175mg; Calcium 291mg; Fibre 2.5g; Sodium 534mg.

**PAGE 28 Lemon and Blueberry Cake** Energy 967kcal/4069kJ; Protein 9.5g; Carbohydrate 150.7g, of which sugars 103.1g; Fat 40.6g, of which saturates 24.5g; Cholesterol 175mg; Calcium 286mg; Fibre 4.4g; Sodium 537mg.

**PAGE 30 Chocolate Chip Marshmallow Cake** Energy 1286kcal/5401kJ; Protein 18.9g; Carbohydrate 175g, of which sugars 125.1g; Fat 61.6g, of which saturates 37.2g; Cholesterol 178mg; Calcium 342mg; Fibre 7.7g; Sodium 745mg.

**PAGE 32 Red Velvet Cake** Energy 1408kcal/5910kJ; Protein 10.5g; Carbohydrate 193.8g, of which sugars 148.3g; Fat 71.1g, of which saturates 43.8g; Cholesterol 246mg; Calcium 317mg; Fibre 2.5g; Sodium 753mg.

**PAGE 34 Coffee and Walnut Cake** Energy 1208kcal/5069kJ; Protein 14.1g; Carbohydrate 160.8g, of which sugars 115.3g; Fat 61g, of which saturates 26.8g; Cholesterol 175mg; Calcium 315mg; Fibre 3.9g; Sodium 544mg.

**PAGE 36 Carrot Cake** Energy 1233kcal/5183kJ; Protein 11g; Carbohydrate 182.8g, of which sugars 137.6g; Fat 56.1g, of which saturates 34.2g; Cholesterol 210mg; Calcium 361mg; Fibre 4.3g; Sodium 673mg.

**PAGE 38 Rocky Road Cake** Energy 1229kcal/5165kJ; Protein 16.1g; Carbohydrate 173g, of which sugars 122.9g; Fat 57.4g, of which saturates 34.6g; Cholesterol 177mg; Calcium 341mg; Fibre 7.6g; Sodium 738mg.

**PAGE 44 Pineapple Upside Down Pudding** Energy 1052kcal/4406kJ; Protein 13.9g; Carbohydrate 128.9g, of which sugars 98.4g; Fat 57g, of which saturates 25.8g; Cholesterol 175mg; Calcium 284mg; Fibre 2g; Sodium 548mg.

**PAGE 46 Sticky Toffee Pudding** Energy 1810kcal/7549kJ; Protein 13.4g; Carbohydrate 171g, of which sugars 140.5g; Fat 124g, of which saturates 68.7g; Cholesterol 276mg; Calcium 329mg; Fibre 2.5g; Sodium 727mg.

**PAGE 48 Sponge Pudding with Jam, Syrup or Lemon Curd** Energy 1020kcal/4273kJ; Protein 14.1g; Carbohydrate 120.4g, of which sugars 89.9g; Fat 57g, of which saturates 25.8g; Cholesterol 175mg; Calcium 290mg; Fibre 1.7g; Sodium 546mg.

**PAGE 50 Ginger Sponge Cake** Energy 1113kcal/4693kJ; Protein 9.9g; Carbohydrate 188.2g, of which sugars 140.5g; Fat 40.9g, of which saturates 24.6g; Cholesterol 176mg; Calcium 292mg; Fibre 2.5g; Sodium 581mg.

**PAGE 52 Upside Down Plum Cake** Energy 958kcal/4034kJ; Protein 10.1g; Carbohydrate 147.7g, of which sugars 103.1g; Fat 40.6g, of which saturates 24.5g; Cholesterol 175mg; Calcium 338mg; Fibre 4.1g; Sodium 536mg.

**PAGE 54 Molten Lava Choc** Energy 1182kcal/4956kJ; Protein 16.1g; Carbohydrate 150.1g, of which sugars 102.7g; Fat 61.6g, of which saturates 37.2g; Cholesterol 178mg; Calcium 329mg; Fibre 7.7g; Sodium 726mg.

**PAGE 56 Baked Alaska** Energy 1190kcal/5008kJ; Protein 18.4g; Carbohydrate 176.2g, of which sugars 128.6g; Fat 50.7g, of which saturates 30.7g; Cholesterol 189mg; Calcium 385mg; Fibre 5.7g; Sodium 822mg.

**PAGE 62 Banana and Walnut Pretzel Cake** Energy 1195kcal/5010kJ; Protein 14.9g; Carbohydrate 155.3g, of which sugars 105.7g; Fat 61.3g, of which saturates 26.8g; Cholesterol 175mg; Calcium 324mg; Fibre 4.5g; Sodium 623mg.

**PAGE 64 Toffee Apple Cake** Energy 1052kcal/4421kJ; Protein 15.9g; Carbohydrate 152g, of which sugars 107.4g; Fat 46.6g, of which saturates 27.1g; Cholesterol 308mg; Calcium 417mg; Fibre 4.1g; Sodium 609mg.

**PAGE 66 Pear and Chocolate Cake** Energy 982kcal/4121kJ; Protein 14.1g; Carbohydrate 129.1g, of which sugars 82.1g; Fat 49.1g, of which saturates 29.6g; Cholesterol 176mg; Calcium 322mg; Fibre 8.4g; Sodium 726mg.

**PAGE 68 Cranberry and Clementine Cake** Energy 950kcal/3999kJ; Protein 10.1g; Carbohydrate 145.5g, of which sugars 100.9g; Fat 40.5g, of which saturates 24.5g; Cholesterol 175mg; Calcium 307mg; Fibre 4.2g; Sodium 536mg.

**PAGE 70 Raspberry and Almond Cream Cake** Energy 948kcal/3968kJ; Protein 15g; Carbohydrate 99.9g, of which sugars 69.4g; Fat 57.2g, of which saturates 25.9g; Cholesterol 175mg; Calcium 302mg; Fibre 4g; Sodium 467mg.

**PAGE 72 Cherry and Vanilla Sponge Cake** Energy 1168kcal/4889kJ; Protein 11.1g; Carbohydrate 137.8g, of which sugars 93.3g; Fat 67.4g, of which saturates 41.2g; Cholesterol 243mg; Calcium 322mg; Fibre 3.7g; Sodium 545mg.

**PAGE 74 Strawberry Layer Cake** Energy 1156kcal/4832kJ; Protein 10.7g; Carbohydrate 122.6g, of which sugars 78g; Fat 72.7g, of which saturates 44.5g; Cholesterol 257mg; Calcium 318mg; Fibre 2.8g; Sodium 552mg.

**PAGE 80 Gin and Lemon Drizzle Cake** Energy 965kcal/4059kJ; Protein 9.5g; Carbohydrate 141.5g, of which sugars 96.5g; Fat 40.5g, of which saturates 24.5g; Cholesterol 175mg; Calcium 285mg; Fibre 2.5g; Sodium 536mg.

**PAGE 82 Mocha Choco with Espresso** Energy 1582kcal/6653kJ; Protein 13.4g; Carbohydrate 241g, of which sugars 192.6g; Fat 69.5g, of which saturates 42.7g; Cholesterol 239mg; Calcium 319mg; Fibre 5.7g; Sodium 922mg.

**PAGE 84 Salted Caramel Pudding** Energy 1866kcal/7783kJ; Protein 17.3g; Carbohydrate 175.8g, of which sugars 130.4g; Fat 126.4g, of which saturates 69.3g; Cholesterol 353mg; Calcium 410mg; Fibre 2.5g; Sodium 1808mg.

**PAGE 86 Pistachio and White Chocolate Cake** Energy 1250kcal/5231kJ; Protein 19g; Carbohydrate 138.7g, of which sugars 93.3g; Fat 72.7g, of which saturates 35.3g; Cholesterol 175mg; Calcium 441mg; Fibre 5.1g; Sodium 756mg.

**PAGE 88 Black and White Chocolate Cake** Energy 1213kcal/5087kJ; Protein 15.1g; Carbohydrate 155.3g, of which sugars 106.8g; Fat 63.4g, of which saturates 38.8g; Cholesterol 217mg; Calcium 326mg; Fibre 7.3g; Sodium 944mg.

**PAGE 90 Irish Cream Liqueur Cake** Energy 1368kcal/5707kJ; Protein 9.8g; Carbohydrate 127.4g, of which sugars 82.8g; Fat 86.7g, of which saturates 53.7g; Cholesterol 264mg; Calcium 307mg; Fibre 2.5g; Sodium 784mg.

**PAGE 92 Whisky and Marmalade Syrup Cake** Energy 1121kcal/4724kJ; Protein 9.6g; Carbohydrate 182.8g, of which sugars 138.2g; Fat 40.5g, of which saturates 24.5g; Cholesterol 175mg; Calcium 307mg; Fibre 2.7g; Sodium 573mg.

**PAGE 98 Marshmallow Cake** Energy 911kcal/3832kJ; Protein 10.6g; Carbohydrate 134.7g, of which sugars 84.5g; Fat 40.5g, of which saturates 24.5g; Cholesterol 175mg; Calcium 284mg; Fibre 2.5g; Sodium 541mg.

**PAGE 100 Ice Cream Cakes** Energy 533kcal/2242kJ; Protein 2.6g; Carbohydrate 85.4g, of which sugars 73.7g; Fat 22.5g, of which saturates 14g; Cholesterol 76mg; Calcium 79mg; Fibre 0.6g; Sodium 232mg.

**PAGE 102 Cola Bottle Cake** Energy 1560kcal/6562kJ; Protein 12.9g; Carbohydrate 219.9g, of which sugars 171.9g; Fat 75.8g, of which saturates 46.7g; Cholesterol 250mg; Calcium 302mg; Fibre 5.7g; Sodium 799mg.

**PAGE 104 Peanut Butter Mug Cake** Energy 1056kcal/4419kJ; Protein 18.5g; Carbohydrate 115g, of which sugars 67.8g; Fat 61.2g, of which saturates 29.6g; Cholesterol 175mg; Calcium 298mg; Fibre 2.5g; Sodium 673mg.

**PAGE 106 Chocolate Hazelnut Cake** Energy 1902kcal/7967kJ; Protein 19.8g; Carbohydrate 227.7g, of which sugars 179.8g; Fat 107.8g, of which saturates 38.4g; Cholesterol 219mg; Calcium 342mg; Fibre 7.4g; Sodium 852mg.

**PAGE 108 Pretty Butterfly Cake** Energy 1182kcal/4987kJ; Protein 10.1g; Carbohydrate 207.3g, of which sugars 162.7g; Fat 40.5g, of which saturates 24.5g; Cholesterol 175mg; Calcium 313mg; Fibre 2.5g; Sodium 541mg.

**PAGE 114 Bonfire Treacle Cake** Energy 1144kcal/4792kJ; Protein 11g; Carbohydrate 142g, of which sugars 90.3g; Fat 63.2g, of which saturates 38.1g; Cholesterol 224mg; Calcium 441mg; Fibre 2.5g; Sodium 797mg.

**PAGE 116 Pumpkin Pie Cake** Energy 1153kcal/4848kJ; Protein 12.1g; Carbohydrate 175.2g, of which sugars 130.1g; Fat 49.9g, of which saturates 30.1g; Cholesterol 175mg; Calcium 407mg; Fibre 2.7g; Sodium 572mg.

**PAGE 118 Halloween Cake** Energy 1891kcal/7933kJ; Protein 11.8g; Carbohydrate 255.7g, of which sugars 209.6g; Fat 98.4g, of which saturates 61g; Cholesterol 305mg; Calcium 324mg; Fibre 3.5g; Sodium 919mg.

**PAGE 120 Christmas Pudding Cake** Energy 1314kcal/5520kJ; Protein 12.9g; Carbohydrate 189.6g, of which sugars 132.6g; Fat 58.7g, of which saturates 32.3g; Cholesterol 234mg; Calcium 345mg; Fibre 2.5g; Sodium 778mg.

**PAGE 122 Chocolate Log** Energy 962.5kcal/4036kJ; Protein 10.7g; Carbohydrate 121.8g, of which sugars 95.4g; Fat 51.6g, of which saturates 31.8g; Cholesterol 152mg; Calcium 196mg; Fibre 6.1g; Sodium 743.5mg.

**PAGE 124 Happy Birthday Cake** Energy 1411kcal/5921kJ; Protein 12.7g; Carbohydrate 189.8g, of which sugars 144.6g; Fat 72.1g, of which saturates 44.1g; Cholesterol 231mg; Calcium 381mg; Fibre 2.8g; Sodium 716mg.

# INDEX

# ACKNOWLEDGEMENTS

This edition is published by Lorenz Books,
an imprint of Anness Publishing Ltd,
108 Great Russell Street,
London WC1B 3NA;
info@anness.com

www.lorenzbooks.com; www.annesspublishing.com;
twitter: @Anness_Books

If you like the images in this book and would
like to investigate using them for publishing,
promotions or advertising, please visit our website
www.practicalpictures.com for more information.

© Anness Publishing Ltd 2015

A CIP catalogue record for this book is available from
the British Library.

Publisher: Joanna Lorenz
Photographer: Clare Winfield
Food Stylist: Rachel Wood
Prop Stylist: Wei Tong
Designer: Adelle Mahoney
Editorial: Sarah Lumby

COOK'S NOTES
For all recipes, quantities are given in both metric and imperial
measures and, where appropriate, in standard cups and spoons.
Follow one set of measures, but not a mixture, because they are
not interchangeable. Standard spoon and cup measures are level.
1 tsp = 5ml, 1 tbsp = 15ml, 1 cup = 250ml/8fl oz.
Australian standard tablespoons are 20ml. Australian readers
should use 3 tsp in place of 1 tbsp for measuring small quantities.
American pints are 16fl oz/2 cups. American readers should use
20fl oz/2.5 cups in place of 1 pint when measuring liquids.
Medium (US large) eggs are used unless otherwise stated.

PUBLISHER'S NOTE
Although the advice and information in this book are believed to
be accurate and true at the time of going to press, neither the
authors nor the publisher can accept any legal responsibility or
liability for any errors or omissions that may have been made nor
for any inaccuracies nor for any loss, harm or injury that comes
about from following instructions or advice in this book.